A Book of Valor

A Collection of the Prose and Poetry
of Old Lands beyond the Sea

By

SISTER M. THOMAS AQUINAS, O.P., M.A.
SISTER M. EILEEN, O.P., M.A.

and

KATHERINE RANKIN

IN ACCORDANCE WITH THE EDUCATIONAL PLAN OF
RIGHT REVEREND GEORGE JOHNSON, PH.D.

AND

UNDER THE GENERAL SUPERVISION OF
MOST REVEREND FRANCIS J. HAAS, D.D., PH.D., LL.D.

AND

RIGHT REVEREND FREDERICK G. HOCHWALT, PH.D.

GINN AND COMPANY

BOSTON · NEW YORK · CHICAGO · ATLANTA · DALLAS
COLUMBUS · SAN FRANCISCO · TORONTO · LONDON

Acknowledgments

For kind permission to reprint copyrighted material, acknowledgment is hereby made to the following:

Appleton-Century-Crofts, Inc., and the author for the selection from *Master Skylark* (copyright, 1896, 1924), by JOHN BENNETT.

Harcourt, Brace and Company, Inc., for "Going up to London," from *Magpie Lane*, by NANCY BYRD TURNER (copyright, 1927, by Harcourt, Brace and Company, Inc.).

Harper & Brothers for "Ill-Luck and the Fiddler," from *Twilight Land*, by HOWARD PYLE (copyright, 1894, by Harper & Brothers; copyright, 1922, by Anna Poole Pyle); "On Christmas Eve," from *In This Our Day*, by EDITH LOVEJOY PIERCE (copyright, 1933, 1938–1944, by the author); both used by permission of Harper & Brothers.

J. B. Lippincott Company, Wm. Blackwood and Sons, Ltd., and the author for "A Song of Sherwood," reprinted from *Collected Poems in One Volume*, by ALFRED NOYES (copyright, 1906, 1934, by Alfred Noyes), reprinted by permission of the publishers, J. B. Lippincott Company.

The Macmillan Company for "The Golden City of Saint Mary," from *Poems*, by JOHN MASEFIELD (copyright, 1913, by Harper & Brothers; 1914, The Century Company and by the McClure Publications; 1912, 1913, 1914, by The Macmillan Company; 1915, 1923, 1924, 1926, 1930, 1931, 1932, 1935, by John Masefield); "O'Connell Bridge," from *The Rocky Road to Dublin*, by JAMES STEPHENS (copyright, 1915, by The Macmillan Company); "Franciscan Aspiration," from "Litany of Heroes" in *Collected Poems*, by VACHEL LINDSAY (copyright, 1923, by The Macmillan Company); all used by permission of The Macmillan Company, publishers.

Macmillan & Co., Ltd., for "O'Connell Bridge," from *The Rocky Road to Dublin*, by JAMES STEPHENS.

Rinehart & Company, Inc., for "A Christmas Folk-Song," from *The Selected Poems of Lizette Woodworth Reese* (copyright, 1926, by Lizette Woodworth Reese), reprinted by permission of Rinehart & Company, Inc., Publishers, New York.

Charles Scribner's Sons for "The Sword Excalibur," from *The Story of King Arthur and His Knights*, by HOWARD PYLE; "Four Things," reprinted from *The Builders and Other Poems*, by HENRY VAN DYKE (copyright, 1897, by Charles Scribner's Sons; 1924, by Henry van Dyke), used by permission of the publishers.

Benziger Brothers, Inc., for "Mother and I in the May," from *Ballads of Childhood*, by REV. MICHAEL EARLS.

The Book House for Children for "Cuculain, the Irish Hound" and "The Homecoming of Odysseus," as retold by OLIVE BEAUPRÉ MILLER in *My Book House*, published by The Book House for Children, Chicago, Illinois.

Curtis Brown, Ltd., and the author for "Saint Jerome and the Lion," from *Beasts and Saints*, by HELEN WADDELL (copyright, 1934, by Henry Holt & Company, Inc.).

[Continued on page vi]

iii

Faith and Freedom
LITERARY READERS

Nibil Obstat:
JAMES J. KORTENDICK, M.A., S.T.B., *Censor Deputatus*

Imprimatur:
☩PATRICK A. O'BOYLE, *Archbishop of Washington*
WASHINGTON, FEBRUARY 13, 1948

COMMISSION		THE
ON		CATHOLIC
AMERICAN		UNIVERSITY
CITIZENSHIP		OF AMERICA

MOST REV. BISHOP PATRICK J. McCORMICK
PRESIDENT OF THE COMMISSION

MARY SYNON, LL.D.	**MOST REV. BISHOP FRANCIS J. HAAS**
EDITORIAL CONSULTANT	CHAIRMAN, EXECUTIVE COMMITTEE
SISTER MARY JOAN, O.P.	**REV. THOMAS OWEN MARTIN**
CURRICULUM CONSULTANT	DIRECTOR

PUBLISHED FOR THE CATHOLIC UNIVERSITY OF AMERICA PRESS
WASHINGTON, D. C.

Preface

This is a Book of Valor.

Within it are stories of brave saints and martyrs, of prophets and pilgrims, of heroes and soldiers. Within it, in its everlasting glory, is the greatest story of valor that the world has ever known, the story of the Child who came to save mankind.

The telling of hero stories is an old, old art. Long before they were set down in writing these tales were passed down from one generation to the next as fathers told their sons. People of many of the older lands knew not only their own stories of national heroes, but those of other races. For two great movements had spread their telling: the pilgrimages to shrines of the Mother of Christ and the Crusades.

The pilgrimages were, for the most part, national, although pilgrims from all over Europe visited the shrines at Bethlehem, at Nazareth, at Jerusalem.

Englishmen went to Walsingham, that ivy-covered chapel of Our Lady.

Irishmen sought grace at the Shrine of Our Lady of Grace in Munster.

Italians knelt in the dust of Pompeii to ask Mary's aid.

Spaniards walked over cold mountains and hot plains to petition Our Lady of the Pillar at Saragossa.

French gypsies journeyed deep into marshland to the Shrine of Saintes Marie.

Austrians thronged to Vienna to pray at the shrine of Mary, Help of Christians.

Germans from Bavaria and Saxony, from Prussia and the Palatinate, united at Freiburg to ask the aid of Our Lady of the Lilies.

The Crusades, greatest of pilgrimages, made their followers storytellers as well as soldiers of Christ. Men came back from the Holy Land steeped in tales of the roads they had traveled, the people they had seen. When they returned to their homes they told stories of these far lands to their children. Out of these tellings grew a great period of art and literature which still enriches the world.

This Book of Valor, setting down traditional tales of many

lands, is necessarily a limited collection. Its selections have been made for their significance, as well as for their literary merit. The fairy tales are only a few of the thousands that have always delighted children. The myths and folklore are tiny segments of a great literary tradition.

The courage of Hector and the daring of Odysseus merely hint at the wealth of Greek literature.

The Christian stories, many and vivid though they are, stand out only as symbols of countless other Christian tales of valor.

If this book brings to its reader glimpses of that valor, it will have accomplished its purpose. For with this courage, inspired by the sublime heroism of Christ, the followers of Christ have done brave deeds. Martyrs and missionaries, pilgrims and Crusaders, kings and peasants, soldiers and saints, following the fortitude of the Man who died upon a Cross, have set their own names in letters of gold upon the pages of immortal fame.

[Continued from page iii]

PADRAIC COLUM for "The Seven Sleepers of Ephesus," from his volume, *The Forge in the Forest*; the executors of the estate of Wilfrid Meynell for "Little Jesus," by FRANCIS THOMPSON; GEORGENE FAULKNER (The Story Lady), for "Cornelia's Jewels"; GERALD M. C. FITZGERALD, C.S.C., for his poem "A Street in Nazareth"; MONK GIBBON for his poem "French Peasants"; Doris Long for "The Little Bells of Sevilla," by DORA SIGERSON SHORTER; Seumas MacManus and M. H. Gill and Son, Dublin, for "The Passing of the Gael," from *Four Winds of Eirinn* by ETHNA CARBERY; Virgil Markham for "How the Great Guest Came," by EDWIN MARKHAM; BRIAN O'HIGGINS for his poem "I Sing the Joy of Christmas"; VIOLET ALLEYN STOREY for her poem "To a Swiss Tune"; Lorna Gill Walsh for the translation by THOMAS WALSH of "For a Blind Beggar's Sign," by CLEMENTE BIONDI, from *Catholic Anthology, the World's Great Catholic Poetry*, edited by Thomas Walsh and published by The Macmillan Company; WILLARD WATTLES for his poem "Gabriel"; ELLA YOUNG for her poem "The Wind from the West."

For their willing assistance acknowledgment is also made to the Faculty of The Catholic University of America; to the Director of the Mullen Library, Mr. Eugene P. Willging, and to the Staffs of the Preparations and Circulation Rooms; to the staff of the Department of Library Science, and particularly to Sister M. Fides, S.N.D.; to the Library Director and the Staff of the Dominican House of Studies; to Sister M. Yvonne, O.P.; and to the Staff of the Reading Room of the Library of Congress.

Grateful acknowledgment is also made to Sister Mary Hildegarde, R.S.M., of Our Lady of Cincinnati College for the choral speech work, and to Mary Frances Sizer for supervision of the requests for use of all copyrighted material.

Contents

A Book of Valor

At Walsingham in England an Augustinian abbot was hanged outside the gates of his priory for opposing the suppression of his monastery by King Henry VIII.
Then the rest of his community were compelled to remove the statue of Our Lady, which had been enshrined there for nearly five hundred years.
Now, after centuries, Walsingham is destined to take its place once more in English Catholic life. For Pope Leo XIII granted the old spiritual privileges to the founder of the Guild of Our Lady of Ransom and, with the restoration of the ancient Slipper Chapel of the shrine, Catholics again are making pilgrimage there.
Kings and their knights once knelt in prayer before Our Lady; but during the Second World War the road that led to Walsingham was filled with khaki-garbed American soldiers, with Poles in exile in England, and with Englishmen and English women who through time and oppression had preserved the faith of their fathers.

Prayer of the Pilgrims at Walsingham

Hail, holy Queen, Mother of mercy, hail, our life, our sweetness, and our hope. To thee do we cry, poor banished children of Eve; to thee do we send up our sighs, mourning and weeping in this vale of tears. Turn then, most gracious Advocate, thine eyes of mercy toward us, and after this our exile, show unto us the blessed fruit of thy womb, Jesus. O clement, O loving, O sweet Virgin Mary!

The White Thorn of Glastonbury

FRANCES JENKINS OLCOTT

There is a golden legend and it relates how Joseph of Arimathea[1]—that good man and just, who laid Our Lord in his own tomb, was persecuted by Pontius Pilate, and how he fled from Jerusalem carrying with him the Holy Grail hidden beneath a cloth of heavy silk, mystical and white.

For many months he wandered, leaning on his staff cut from a white-thorn bush. He passed over raging seas and dreary wastes; he wandered through trackless forests, climbed rugged mountains, and forded many floods. At last he came to where the Apostle Philip was preaching the glad tidings to the heathen. And there Joseph abode[2] for a little while.

Now, upon a night while Joseph lay asleep in his hut, he was wakened by a radiant light. And as he gazed with wondering eyes he saw an angel standing by his couch, wrapped in a cloud of incense.

"Joseph of Arimathea," said the angel, "cross thou over into Britain and preach the glad tidings to the king. And there do thou build the first Christian church in that land."

While Joseph lay there silent, wondering in his heart what answer he should make, the angel vanished from his sight.

Then Joseph left his hut and, calling the Apostle Philip, gave him the angel's message. When morning dawned, Philip sent him on his way, accompanied by eleven chosen

1. *Arimathea* (ăr ĭ mà thē'ä).　　2. *abode* (à bōd'): stayed, dwelt.

12

followers. To the water's side they went, and embarking in a little ship, they came unto the coast of Britain.

And they were met there by the heathen who carried them before their king. To him and to his people did Joseph of Arimathea preach the glad tidings; but the king's heart, though moved, was not convinced. Nevertheless he gave to Joseph and his eleven followers Avalon,[3] the happy isle, the isle of the blessed, and he bade them depart straightway and build there an altar to their God.

A wonderful gift was this same Avalon, sometimes called the Island of Apples, and also known to the people of the land as the Isle of Glassy Waters. Beautiful and peaceful was it. Deep it lay in the midst of a green valley, and the balmy breezes fanned its apple orchards and scattered afar the sweet fragrance of rosy blossoms and ripened fruit. Soft grew the green grass beneath the feet. The smooth waves gently lapped the shore, and water lilies floated on the surface of the tide while in the blue sky above sailed the fleecy clouds.

It was on a holy day that Joseph and his companions reached the Isle of Avalon. With them they carried the Holy Grail hidden beneath its cloth of snow-white silk. Heavily the little company toiled up the steep hill called Weary-All. When they reached the top Joseph halted and thrust his pilgrim's staff of white-thorn into the ground.

And, lo! a miracle! the thorn-staff put forth roots, sprouted and budded. Then while Joseph stood lost in wonder the buds opened and the staff was covered with a mass of white blossoms—and the blossoms were so sweet

3. *Avalon* (ăv'à lŏn).

the air was filled with the fragrance of them. And on the spot where the thorn had bloomed, there Joseph built the first Christian church in Britain. He made it "wattled all round"[4] of willows gathered from the water's edge. Then in the chapel they placed the Holy Grail.

And so, it is said, ever since at Glastonbury Abbey— the name by which Avalon is known today—on that same holy day the white-thorn buds and blooms. *Adapted from William of Malmesbury and other sources*

4. *"wattled all round"*: willows woven together to form a framework.

Our Lord and Our Lady

HILAIRE BELLOC

[Choir to be arranged in three voices: high, medium, and low.]

High They warned Our Lady for the Child
That was Our blessed Lord,
Medium, low And she took Him into the desert wild,
Over the camel's ford.

High And a long song she sang to Him
And a short story told:
Medium, low And she wrapped Him in a woolen cloak
To keep Him from the cold.

Medium But when Our Lord was grown a man
The rich they dragged Him down,
Low And they crucified Him in Golgotha,
Out and beyond the town.

Medium They crucified Him on Calvary
Upon an April day;
High, medium And because He had been her little Son
She followed Him all the way.

Low Our Lady stood beside the Cross
A little space apart,
Medium And when she heard Our Lord cry out
All A sword went through her heart.

Medium They laid Our Lord in a marble tomb,
Low Dead in a winding sheet,
All But Our Lady stands above the world
With the white moon at her feet.

The Knight of Bethlehem

HENRY NEVILLE MAUGHAM

There was a Knight of Bethlehem
Whose wealth was tears and sorrows;
His men-at-arms were little lambs,
His trumpeters were sparrows.
His castle was a wooden cross,
On which He hung so high;
His helmet was a crown of thorns,
Whose crest did reach the sky.

Crusader's Song

JOSEPHINE DASKAM BACON

Above our heads, against the blue,
The banner floats like foam:
Reddened and soiled and torn 'twill be,
Ere we again come home!

Full many leagues have we to go,
Full many lands to roam;
And some must march beyond this world,
Ere we again come home!

Behind us lie our castle walls,
Before, the swelling dome;
But some shall fill a narrow house,
Ere we again come home!

The love of England goes with us,
A blessing comes from Rome;
But some shall God in heaven greet,
Ere we again come home!

Five great highways once led through Ireland
to the ancient court of Tara. Now the Druids[1] and the kings
who traveled that road are gone, but ever-burning
is the faith that Saint Patrick kindled at Tara
when he lighted

The Paschal Fire

THOMAS QUINN BEESLY

It was in the springtime that Patrick and his companions landed on the shores of Ireland. At first the Druids resisted him, but Patrick had his mission too deeply at heart to be discouraged by opposition. He traveled along the coast until at the mouth of the Boyne he found a more friendly people. There he began his preaching of the Word. There, too, he learned that the chieftains of Ireland had been summoned by the most powerful of the Irish kings to celebrate a special feast at Tara. In this celebration Patrick instantly saw a wonderful opportunity to overthrow the power of the Druids. He determined to be there.

It was on Easter Sunday that the great meeting was to take place. The king issued an order that, under pain of death, all the fires throughout the kingdom should be put out on the day before Easter, and that no fire should be lighted anywhere until the signal blaze was kindled at the royal palace.

All the chieftains were present, and the Druids had summoned all their forces, for they had heard of Patrick and they knew that he had come to overthrow their power forever.

1. *Druids:* members of a pagan religious order in ancient Ireland.

Patrick arrived on Easter Saturday at a hill on the opposite side of the valley from the royal palace. On Easter Eve he kindled the Paschal fire on the top of the hill.

The Druid priests were amazed at the daring of this Christian, and they were also alarmed because of an old prophecy which had been made centuries before: "The fire which has been lighted in defiance of the royal order will blaze forever in the land, unless it be darkened before the dawn."

They hurried to the king and reminded him of the prophecy. A frown clouded his face as he listened, and at the end he burst out angrily, "We will go at once and put out the fire and slay the man who dares to defy our authority." And the king with nine chariots filled with his chieftains and the two chief Druids went at once to the hill on which Patrick had lighted the Paschal fire.

When they drew near the place, one of the Druids cried out, "O King, thou shalt not go to the place where the fire is, lest perhaps thou shouldst afterwards adore him who has kindled it. But this man shall be summoned before thee that he may learn to obey thee. And we and he shall debate together in thy presence, O King, and thou shalt decide between us."

The king answered, "Your counsel is good; be it done as you say."

So Patrick was summoned before the king and the Druids said to their followers, "Do not stand up at his coming, for whosoever shall stand up at his coming will hereafter believe in him and adore him."

Patrick approached the king singing in a loud, clear voice the hymn of the Psalmist David, "Some trust in chariots and some in horses, but we will call on the name of the Lord our God."

The king and his chieftains were seated in a half circle with their shields held before them and reaching up to their chins. Only one among them dared to disobey the order of the Druid priest. He stood up to do honor to this fearless Christian, and Patrick blessed him and he was converted at that very moment.

One of the Druids then broke forth in insults upon Patrick and said many wicked things about Our Savior and about the practices of Christians.

Patrick defied him to his face. He lifted his voice in prayer: "Let God arise and let His enemies be scattered and let those who hate Him fly before His face."

Immediately a great darkness came down upon them, and the multitude of heathens became confused and fell upon each other and at once there came a great earthquake, and the horses with the chariots fled over the plain, leaving many men dead. Drochan, the Druid High Priest, fearing that the anger of Patrick would cause the death of the king, ran to him and, throwing himself on his knees, cried out, "O righteous and mighty man, do not destroy the king. He will come and bend the knee to thee and worship thy God."

And the king, in fear and trembling, approached Patrick and bent his knee before him.

On the next day, which was Easter Sunday, Patrick, dressed in his bishop's robes with his mitre and crozier, marched in procession with his companions to the palace. The Druids were filled with fear and anger; they feared that the miracles which Patrick had worked the night before would cause all the people to turn away from them and go to Patrick. They were angry that Patrick had greater powers than they. So the chief Druid, Drochan, challenged Patrick to work wonders on the great plain.

Patrick asked, "What wonders?"

And Drochan said, "Let us bring down snow upon the ground."

Patrick said, "I do not wish to act contrary to the will of God."

And Drochan, boasting, said, "I will bring snow down in sight of all the people."

And, by magical spells, he caused the whole plain to be covered with snow to the height of a man's waist. And the crowd beheld this and wondered at the power of the Druid.

Then Patrick said, "Lo, now we see the snow; take it away."

And Drochan answered, "I cannot take it away until this same hour tomorrow."

Patrick said, "You can do evil, but you cannot do good. It is not so with me."

Then he blessed the plain, and no sooner were his words spoken than the snow disappeared without wind or rain. And the people shouted for joy and were filled with wonder at the power possessed by this Christian who feared neither the king nor the Druid High Priest.

Drochan made another attempt to show his power. Appealing to the Evil One, he brought down a great darkness upon the earth. Patrick challenged him to remove it, but he could not. And when he had tried in

vain, then Patrick prayed, and the darkness was immediately dispelled and the sun shone forth. And all the multitude gave thanks to God for the wonderful power which He had shown in their midst.

After this Patrick worked many more miracles. And the influence of the Druid priests over the people was broken on that day. Patrick and his companions instructed and baptized a great many of the assembled multitude.

And from that Easter Sunday until the day of his death, Patrick traveled throughout Ireland working miracles, preaching the word of God, and receiving into the Church, through baptism, multitudes of the Irish people. The land became known thereafter as the Island of Saints and Scholars, and the children of Ireland, in all their wanderings throughout the world, have always held in loving remembrance the name of Patrick, the Saint and the Apostle of Ireland.

St. Patrick's Hymn before Tara

Translated by JAMES CLARENCE MANGAN

At Tara today, in this fateful hour,
I place all heaven with its power,
And the sun with its brightness,
And the snow with its whiteness,
And fire with all the strength it hath,
And lightning with its rapid wrath,
And the winds with their swiftness along their path,
And the sea with its deepness,
And the rocks with their steepness,
And the earth with its starkness,—
    All these I place,
    By God's almighty help and grace,
Between myself and the powers of darkness.

    At Tara today
    May God be my stay!
May the strength of God now nerve me!
May the power of God preserve me!
May God the Almighty be near me!
May God the Almighty espy me!
May God the Almighty hear me!
May God give me eloquent speech!
May the arm of God protect me!
May God give me power to teach and to preach!

May the shield of God defend me!
May the host of God attend me!
    And ward me,
    And guard me!

The Son of God was born in a stable at Bethlehem.
First to worship Him were the animals, the ox and the ass.
After them came the shepherds, dazed by the light of the Star
and the words of the Angel. "Fear not, for behold I bring you
tidings of great joy . . . Glory to God in the highest
and on earth peace to men of good will."
Then the wise men, their camels weighted with gifts,
journeyed to see a King. They found the Christ Child.
Ever since the Star lighted the way to the little town
of Bethlehem the place of the birth of Christ has been
holy ground. The mighty of the earth have traveled long roads
to pay homage to a Child born in poverty. In tribute to Him
and to His Blessed Mother they say the great prayer of faith,
the

Prayer of the Pilgrims at Bethlehem

Hail, Mary, full of grace, the Lord is with thee; blessed art thou amongst women, and blessed is the fruit of thy womb, Jesus. Holy Mary, Mother of God, pray for us sinners, now and at the hour of our death. Amen.

Christmas Eve, with all its joy and beauty, carried
with it a vision of things to come to the little dog
who watched the Christ Child

All Through the Night

RACHEL FIELD

All that day the inn yard had been thronged with
people coming to pay their taxes in the town of Bethlehem.
The small sturdy watchdog who slept in the stable and
picked up what food he could find had never before seen
such a crowd of travelers.

When night fell he was tired from barking at so many
strangers and their beasts and with scurrying out of the
way of feet and hoofs. But, for all the barking and running about, it had been a good day. The inn had over-
flowed into the yard. There had been a fire there with
meat roasting over it and pots that sent out clouds of
savory steam. Many a rich morsel had fallen his way,
so he felt well content as he crept into his corner of the
stable near the oxen's stall.

Night was coming fast and all the birds and beasts
and insects of the stable knew that it belonged to them.
The world was theirs as the world of day could never
be. When the sun rose, man would be their master again.
They would carry his burdens or feed or serve him according to their different gifts. But night was their own. It
was good that this should be so, the little dog thought,
as he burrowed deeper into the straw.

His sworn enemy, the cat, slid by. She moved like a
shadow with fiery-green eyes ready to pounce upon the

mice who were already squeaking and scampering at their play. But the dog was too tired and comfortable to give chase, so for once he let her pass. All about him crickets chirped in rusty chorus and sometimes a bat swooped so low he could feel the stir of its wings. The darkness was warm and alive with the familiar scents of fur and feathers and grain and straw.

"Rest well. Rest well. Rest well." The doves cooed sleepily, making a soft sound in their throats that was like the bubbling of a well-filled pot over a fire.

Night had come to Bethlehem. The inn had been full hours ago. The dog could hear late travelers being turned away. The stable door was bolted against intruders, and the wind was rising, frosty and keen. Through an opening in the roof a star shone bright as purest silver.

"I never saw a star look so large or so near," the cock observed as he moved about with his spurred, high-stepping walk. "Somehow it makes me very restless, and there is something strange in the air. Perhaps you have felt it, too?"

But the dog made no answer. He yawned and laid his pointed muzzle on his paws and prepared himself for sleep.

He woke at the sound of voices outside and roused himself to bark. But though the hair rose along his back, no sound came rumbling from his throat. The bolt was drawn and the stable door opened to lantern light and the dim shapes of two men and a donkey on whose back a woman sat, wrapped in a heavy cloak.

"Well"—the voice of the innkeeper sounded short and impatient—"if you cannot go on, there is only the

25

stable to offer. Coming as you have at such an hour, you are fortunate to have this shelter till morning."

"The roads were crowded," the man answered him, "and our pace was slow because of my wife. You can see that she is nearly spent."

"Yes, yes." The innkeeper was already shutting the door. "I am sorry for your plight, but I tell you there is no room left."

The dog was on his feet. He could hear the other animals rising about him, yet not one of them uttered a sound. Their throats were as silent as his own.

In the flickering lantern light he watched the man lift the woman from the donkey's back and set her upon her feet. She was so weary she would have fallen, but for the man's arms.

"Joseph," she said, "you must not be troubled for me."

She rested her head on the man's shoulder and sighed so softly it might have been one of the doves in the rafters.

"But, Mary," the man went on, "it is not right and fitting that you should be here,—not in a stable among the beasts."

"Who knows," she comforted him, "what is to be? These beasts are more kind than men who kill and hurt one another. I am glad to be here. Their warm breath comforts me. Their straw is clean and soft to rest upon."

Everywhere beyond the ring of light that the lantern made, bright eyes were upon the strangers. Furry ears and quivering noses pointed, alert and watchful.

The strange donkey, freed of his load, found a place beside the ass. He sank down, too tired to drink water or reach for a mouthful of hay.

A hush was on the stable. Not only were all throats silent, but no wings stirred; no claws scratched and not a hoof pounded. And in that hour nothing died. The young swallows and mice were safe from their enemies, for a mystery greater than death held them all in its power.

The lantern flickered and went out.

"Our light is gone!" the man cried out in distress.

"There will be light enough." The woman spoke in a faint voice, and as if in answer the star in the roof gap shone brighter than before.

How long it was after that the little dog could not tell. Morning was still far off, yet the cock suddenly lifted up his voice, so shrill and clear it seemed he would split himself in two. It was not like any other cockcrow since the world began, and it rose higher than the rafters and mounted to heaven itself.

At the same instant each creature found voice and

joined with him. Every living thing in the stable had a part in that swelling chorus of praise. Even the bees hummed till their hive throbbed with music, sweeter than all its store of honey.

"What manner of place is this?" the man cried out in wonder. "What beasts are these who have the tongues of angels?"

But the woman answered him softly out of the shadows. "It was they who gave us shelter this night. Let them draw near and be the first to worship."

She drew aside the folds of her cloak, and light filled the stable even to the farthest corners. The dog cowered before such strange brightness. When he dared to look more closely he saw that it encircled the head of an infant, new born.

"There is no bed for Him to lie upon," the man sighed. "Only this"—and he pointed to the manger.

"My heart tells me there will be nights when He will have no place at all to rest His head," the mother said.

So the Child lay quiet in the straw-filled wooden manger, and all the animals came to view Him there—the oxen, the cow, the ass and the donkey, the ewe and her lambs, the gray goat, the dog, the hens and the proud cock ruffling his feathers. The cat left off her prowling to join them, and the mice ran beside her without fear. The crickets came, too, drawn from the comfort of their warm straw; the bees, from their snug hive. The tireless ants and spiders left their toil to draw near. The swallows in the eaves flew down; the bats bent low on their dark wings, and the doves came closest of all with their soft murmurs above the manger. When they had all seen the

Wonder they returned to their places and were quiet again.

All but the dog. He could not rest as he had before. He stretched himself beside the manger and lay with his head on his folded paws, his eyes wide and watchful as the hours passed.

Long before sunrise the door opened without sound of bolt being drawn and a band of shepherds came in. They bore a strange tale on their lips, and they also worshiped on bended knees. One carried a lamb in his arms, and the Child answered its bleating with a smile.

"Behold the Lamb of God," they said one to another as they turned to go back to their flocks on the hills of Judea.

The star grew pale and through the gap in the stable roof morning showed rosy in the east. Even before the cock hailed it, the dog knew that the sun was up. But he did not move lest he rouse the three in his care. It was then that he saw a strange thing.

The rafters high above cast their shadows as the rising sun struck through. Two of the beams crossed in sharp black bars that fell directly across the sleeping Child.

It was a shadow of the Cross.

On Christmas Eve

EDITH LOVEJOY PIERCE

On Christmas eve the ox, the ass, the sheep
Spoke to the Christ Child as He lay asleep.

Said the ass:
"You will carry heavy burdens, little Brother.
Mighty loads will be put upon You, little Brother."

Said the sheep:
"They will shear You of your fleece, little Brother.
They will strip You on a cold day, little Brother."

Said the ox:
"You will draw a plough through stony soil, little Brother.
Wood shall be laid across Your neck, little Brother."

So softly spoke the ox, the ass, the sheep;
They troubled not the little Jesus' sleep.

"While Shepherds Watched Their Flocks by Night"

NAHUM TATE

While shepherds watched their flocks by night,
 All seated on the ground,
The angel of the Lord came down,
 And glory shone around.

"Fear not," said he, for mighty dread
 Had seized their troubled mind;
"Glad tidings of great joy I bring
 To you and all mankind.

"To you, in David's town, this day
 Is born, of David's line,
The Savior, who is Christ the Lord,
 And this shall be the sign:

"The heavenly babe you there shall find
 To human view displayed,
All meanly wrapped in swaddling bands,
 And in a manger laid."

Thus spake the seraph; and forthwith
 Appeared a shining throng
Of angels, praising God, who thus
 Addressed their joyful song:

"All glory be to God on high,
 And to the earth be peace;
Good will henceforth from Heaven to men
 Begin and never cease."

[Choir to be arranged
in three voices:
high, medium, and low.]

A Christmas Folk Song

LIZETTE WOODWORTH REESE

All	The little Jesus came to town;
High	The wind blew up, [Medium] the wind blew down;
Low	Out in the street the wind was bold;
All	Now who would house Him from the cold?
Medium	Then opened wide the stable door,
High	Fair were the rushes on the floor;
Medium	The ox put forth a horned head:
Low	"Come, little Lord, here make Thy bed."
All	Up rose the sheep were folded near;
Medium	"Thou Lamb of God, come, enter here."
Low	He entered there to rush and reed,
All	Who was the Lamb of God indeed.
High	The little Jesus came to town;
Medium	With ox and sheep He laid Him down;
Medium	Peace to the byre, [High, Medium] peace to the fold,
All	For that they housed Him from the cold!

Carol of the Russian Children

RUSSIAN FOLK SONG

Snow-bound mountains, snow-bound valleys,
Snow-bound plateaus, clad in white,
Fur-robed moujiks,[1] fur-robed nobles,
Fur-robed children, see the light.
Shaggy pony, shaggy oxen,
Gentle shepherds wait the light;
Little Jesus, little Mother,
Good Saint Joseph, come this night.

The Three Holy Kings

ALICE ISABEL HAZELTINE

In a far country, in the days before Jesus was born in Judea, there were wise men who studied the heavens by night and by day, for they knew of the prophecy which said that a star shall be born or spring out of Jacob and a man shall arise in the line of Israel. Twelve of them were chosen to watch for the star. Every year they went up a mountain, which was called the Hill of Victory, and for three days they abode there and prayed Our Lord that He would show to them the star.

Now it happened that they were there on the day of the Nativity of Jesus Christ, and a star came over them upon this mountain, which had the form of a right fair child, and under his head was a shining cross, and from this cross came a voice saying, "Today is there born a King in Judea."

Now in a land in which the soil is red with gold, there reigned a king called Melchior. And, where frankincense flows from the trees, the king Balthasar ruled. And in the land where myrrh hangs from the bushes, reigned a third king, called Caspar. These three kings also saw the star and heard the voice, and they each made ready to go on a journey. No one of the three knew that the others intended thus to make a pilgrimage. They gathered together their treasures to present to the king whom they should seek and summoned those who should attend them. So each set out with a great company. And as they journeyed they found the mountains made level as the plains, while the swollen rivers became as dry land.

And never did they lose sight of the star, which shined upon them as the sun, always moving before them to guide them on their way.

But when they were come within two miles of Jerusalem, the star disappeared, a heavy fog arose, and each party halted. Melchior, as it fell out, took his stand on Mount Calvary, Balthasar on the Mount of Olives, and Caspar just between them. When the fog cleared away, each was astonished to see two other great companies besides his own. Then the kings first discovered that all had come upon the same errand, and they embraced with great joy and rode together into Jerusalem.

When they came into the city, Herod and all the people were troubled, because of their so great company like unto an army. Then the three kings demanded in what place the King of the Jews was born, for, said they, "We have seen His star in the Orient, and therefore we come to worship Him."

When Herod had heard this, he was much troubled, and all Jerusalem with him. Then Herod called all the priests of the law, and the doctors, and demanded of them where Jesus Christ should be born. And when he had understood them that He should be born in Bethlehem, Herod called the three kings apart and demanded of them the time that the star had appeared to them. And he said to them that as soon as they should have found the Child and have worshiped Him, that they should return and tell him, pretending that he would worship Him also, though he thought that he would go to slay Him.

As soon as the kings were entered into Jerusalem, the sight of the star was taken from them. But when they were gone out of the city, the star appeared again and went before them, until it came above the place in Bethlehem where the Child was. And they had journeyed now full thirteen days.

When they had entered into the place they worshiped the young Child, and Mary, His mother. Now the kings had brought great treasures with them, but when they had bowed down before the Child, they were filled with fear and amazement because of the so-great light which was in the place. And each offered quickly the first thing that came to his hands and forgot all the other gifts.

Melchior offered thirty golden pennies, Balthasar gave frankincense, and Caspar myrrh; but all else they quite forgot and only remembered that they bowed before the Child and said, "Thanks be to God."

When they would have stayed to do honor to the Holy Child, an angel came to them in a dream to warn them against Herod, who would do them harm. So they departed each to his own country, journeying for two years. And they preached unto the people, telling them of the new-born King, and everywhere upon the temples men placed the figure of a star, the Child, and a cross.

Now it happened years later that Saint Thomas the Apostle journeyed to a far country to preach, and that he wondered why the star was placed upon the temples. Then the priests in those temples told him about the three kings and how they had journeyed to Bethlehem and had seen the young Child.

The three kings were very old and feeble, but when they heard about Saint Thomas, each set out from his own place to go to meet him. When they had come together they built them a city and lived together there for two years, worshiping God and preaching. Then Melchior died and was buried in a large and costly tomb. When Balthasar died, he, too, was buried there. And at last Caspar was placed beside his companions.

Now in the days of Constantine the Great, his mother, Helena, determined to find the bodies of the three kings, and for this she made a journey to the far country. And when she had found them, she brought them to Constantinople to the Church of St. Sophia, where they were held in much honor. And from Constantinople they were taken to Milan, where again many pilgrims came. Now when Frederick Barbarossa[1] laid siege to the city of Milan, he rejoiced above all else to find them there. By him they were taken to Cologne, and there a golden shrine was built in which the bones of the three holy kings were placed that there they might remain until the Judgment Day.

Adapted from The Golden Legend, and other sources

I Sing the Joy of Christmas

BRIAN O'HIGGINS

I sing the joy of Christmas,
Its beauty and its glory,
The splendor of its story,
The wonder of its peace;
I sing the joy of Christmas,
The Virgin Maid who bore Him,
The choirs of angels o'er Him,
The hearts of men aglow.

I sing the joy of Christmas,
The memories it brings us,
The happy songs it sings us
To hold us in its thrall;
I sing the joy of Christmas,
Its streams of grace o'erflowing
Its star of knowledge showing
God's mercy to us all.

1. *Frederick Barbarossa:* German king and emperor at the time of the Crusades.

Words from an Old Spanish Carol

RUTH SAWYER

Shall I tell you who will come
   to Bethlehem on Christmas Morn,
who will kneel them gently down
   before the Lord, new-born?

One small fish from the river,
   with scales of red, red gold,
one wild bee from the heather,
   one gray lamb from the fold,
one ox from the high pasture,
   one black bull from the herd,
one goatling from the far hills,
   one white, white bird.

And many children—God give them grace,
bringing tall candles to light Mary's face.

Shall I tell you who will come
   to Bethlehem on Christmas Morn,
who will kneel them gently down
   before the Lord, new-born?

Little Jesus

FRANCIS THOMPSON

Little Jesus, wast Thou shy
Once, and just so small as I?
And what did it feel like to be
Out of Heaven, and just like me?
Didst Thou sometimes think of *there*,
And ask where all the angels were?
I should think that I would cry
For my house all made of sky;
I would look about the air,
And wonder where my angels were;

And at waking 'twould distress me—
Not an angel there to dress me!
Hadst Thou ever any toys,
Like us little girls and boys?
And didst Thou play in Heaven with all
The angels that were not too tall,
With stars for marbles? Did the things
Play *Can you see me?* through their wings?

Didst Thou kneel at night to pray,
And didst Thou join Thy hands, this way?
And did they tire sometimes, being young,
And make the prayer seem very long?
And dost Thou like it best, that we
Should join our hands to pray to Thee?
I used to think, before I knew,
The prayer not said unless we do.
And did Thy Mother at the night
Kiss Thee, and fold the clothes in right?

And didst Thou feel quite good in bed,
Kissed, and sweet, and Thy prayers said?

Thou canst not have forgotten all
That it feels like to be small.
And Thou knowst I cannot pray
To Thee in my father's way—
When Thou wast so little, say,
Couldst Thou talk Thy Father's way?—

So, a little Child, come down
And hear a child's tongue like Thy own.
Take me by the hand and walk,
And listen to my baby-talk.
To Thy Father show my prayer
(He will look, Thou art so fair),
And say, "O Father, I, Thy Son,
Bring the prayer of a little one."

And He will smile, that children's tongue
Has not changed since Thou wast young!

Beside the River Jordan

The River Jordan flows through old and holy ground. It rises from its source of many springs at the foot of Mount Hermon. Then, between steep banks and deep thickets, it flows southward through the Sea of Galilee and into the Dead Sea.

It is sacred soil because Christ lived in the valley of the Jordan. It is a holy place because Peter preached there and other Apostles trod the chalky roads along the river.

Out of the land of the Jordan has come the greatest of all literature, the story of the birth and life and sufferings and death of Christ. Out of it, too, has come a wealth of legend about Our Lord and about those who served Him.

A legend is a method of storytelling that is older than Christ. It is a survival of old myths of ancient races. It is the expression of simple people. It is a desire to voice their belief in the supernatural. It is a combination of wisdom and fantasy.

A legend always follows the same literary pattern. Christian legends tell of saints who command the elements of water, rain, fire. Animals, wild or the most timid, serve the saints. Bells ring of themselves. Dragons are conquered. Dungeon doors are opened.

Men told legends long before they knew the art of printing them. They told these legends on the heights of Gilead, on the Damascus road, in Roman market places, in the stone quarries of Gaul. The stories are the most primitive ideas of the lives of the saints, but sometimes they are really outgrowths of the genuine history of holy men. The stories survive because of their simple beauty.

In the public square at Nazareth there stands a low arch over a little pool. Today, just as they did nearly two thousand years ago, the women of Nazareth come to the well that is known as "the fountain of Mary."
But Nazareth, though it still remains a little hill town set down among the rocky crags of Galilee, is a shrine for all the world.
Here Jesus played in the workshop of Joseph; here He learned to use the ax and the carpenter's square; here He made things with His holy hands, and helped His Mother, and loved His neighbors, and talked with His friends.
From this little village of Nazareth began the long and tragic journey that would lead Him past the Sea of Galilee, past the height from which He preached the Sermon on the Mount, through the Jaffa Gate, to the dark terror of Calvary.
Now, in the Church of the Annunciation at Nazareth, the faithful remember the beginning of the Way of the Cross, and repeat the

Prayer of the Pilgrims at Nazareth

Queen of Angels, pray for us
Queen of Patriarchs, pray for us
Queen of Prophets, pray for us
Queen of Apostles, pray for us
Queen of Martyrs, pray for us
Queen of Confessors, pray for us
Queen of Virgins, pray for us
Queen of all Saints, pray for us
Queen conceived without original sin, pray for us
Queen of the most holy Rosary, pray for us
Queen of peace, pray for us.

A Legend

ABRAM J. RYAN

He walked alone beside the lonely sea,
The slanting sunbeams fell upon His face,
His shadow fluttered on the pure white sands
Like the weary wing of a soundless prayer.
He wore the seamless robe His mother made—
And as He gathered it about His breast,
The wavelets heard a sweet and gentle voice
Murmur, "Oh! My Mother"—the white sands felt
The touch of tender tears He wept the while
He walked beside the sea;
Sudden, a sea-bird, driven by a storm
That had been sweeping on the farther shore,
Came fluttering towards Him, and, panting, fell
At His feet and died; and then a boy said:
"Poor little bird," in such a piteous tone;
Christ took the bird and laid it in His hand,
And breathed on it—when to his amaze
The little fisher-boy beheld the bird
Flutter a moment and then fly aloft—
Its little life returned; and then he gazed
With look intense upon the wondrous face
(Ah! it was beautiful and fair)—and said:
"Thou art so sweet I wish Thou wert my God."
He leaned down towards the boy and softly said:
"I *am* thy Christ." The day they followed Him
With cross upon His shoulders, to His death,
Within the shadow of a shelt'ring rock
That little boy knelt down, and there adored,
While others cursed the thorn-crowned Crucified.

Saint Jerome and the Lion

TRANSLATED BY HELEN WADDELL

About a mile distant from the River Jordan is a monastery, called after the Abbot Jerome who dwelt there near the holy city of Bethlehem.

Much has been written of his austere life and humble ways, and much has been forgotten. One legend, though, remains immortal; it is the story of the wounded lion and of the help he received from Saint Jerome.

Upon a certain day as evening drew on, the blessed Jerome sat with the brethren, as is the way of the monk, to hear the reading of the lesson and to speak good words. Lo, of a sudden, limping on three paws and the fourth caught up, came a mighty lion into the cloister. At sight of him a good many of the brethren fled in terror, for humans are fearful. But the blessed Jerome went out to meet him as one greets a guest.

While the distance between them was shortening, the lion who had no way of speaking, it not being his nature,

offered the good father as best he might his wounded paw. The saint, calling the brethren, gave instructions that the wounded paw should be bathed to find out why the lion went thus limping. Upon close examination they found that the paw had been pierced by thorns. Herbs were applied with all haste, and the wound speedily healed.

And now, all wildness and savagery laid aside, the lion began to go to and fro among them as peaceable and domestic as any animal about the house. This the blessed Jerome noted and spoke as follows to the brethren: "Bring your minds to bear upon this, my brethren: what, I ask you, can we find for this lion to do? It must be useful and suitable work that will not be burdensome to him. For I believe that it was not so much for the healing of his paw that God sent him hither, since He could have cured him without us, as to show us that He is anxious to provide for us."

To which the brethren gave humble response: "Thou knowest, Father, that the donkey who brings us our wood from the forest pasture needs someone to look after him, and that we are always in fear that some stronger beast will devour him. Wherefore, if it seem to thee good and right, let the charge of our donkey be laid upon the lion, that he may take him out to pasture and again may bring him home."

And so it was done. The lion went with the donkey, as his shepherd. Together they took the road to the pasture, and wherever the donkey grazed, there was his defender; and a sure defence he was. Nevertheless, at regular hours, that he might refresh himself and the donkey might do his appointed task, the lion would come with him home.

And so for long enough it was, till one day, the donkey duly brought to his pasture, the lion felt a great weight of weariness come upon him, and he fell asleep. And as he lay sunk in deep slumber, it befell that certain merchants came along that road on their way to Egypt to buy oil. They saw the donkey grazing, they saw that no guardian was at hand and, seized by sudden wicked greed, they caught him and led him away.

In due course the lion awoke, knowing nothing of his loss, and set out to fetch his charge. But when he was not to be seen in the usual pasture, upset with anxiety and in deep distress, the lion went roaring up and down, hither and thither, for the remainder of the day, seeking what he had lost. And at last, when all hope of finding the donkey was gone, he came and stood at the monastery gate.

Conscious of guilt, he no longer dared walk in as of old time with his donkey. The blessed Jerome saw him, and the brethren too, hanging about outside the gate, without the donkey, and long past his usual hour. They concluded that he had been tempted by hunger to kill his animal. In no mind, therefore, to offer him his usual ration, they cried, "Away with you, and finish up whatever you have left of the donkey, and fill your greed." Yet even as they spoke, they were doubtful as to whether he had indeed done this crime or no.

So finally the brethren went out to the pasture whither the lion was accustomed to bring the donkey, and up and down they scoured to see if they could find any trace of the slaughtered. No sign of violence was to be seen, and turning home they made haste to bring their report to the blessed Jerome.

He heard them and spoke. "I entreat you, brethren," said he, "that although ye have suffered the loss of the ass, do not, nevertheless, nag at the lion or make him wretched. Treat him as before and offer him his food. Let him take the donkey's place and make a light harness for him so that he can drag home the branches that have fallen in the wood." And it was done.

So the lion did regularly his appointed task, while the time drew on for the merchants to return. Then one day, his work done, he went out, inspired as I believe, and made his way to the field. Up and down, hither and thither in circles he ran, craving some further light on the fate that had befallen his comrade. And finally, worn out but still anxious, he climbed to a rising above the highway where he might look all round him. A great way off he spied men coming with laden camels, and in front of them walked a donkey. So far off was he that he could not recognize him. Nonetheless he set out, stepping cautiously, to meet them.

Now it is said to be the custom in that part of the country that whenever men set out with camels on a long journey, a donkey goes in front with the camel's halter on its neck, and the camels follow after. As the merchants came nearer, the lion recognized his donkey. With a fierce roar he charged down upon them, making a mighty din, though doing no damage to any. Crazed with terror, as they well might be, they left all they had and took to their heels, the lion meantime roaring terribly

and lashing the ground with his tail. So he drove the
frightened camels, laden as they were, back to the
monastery before him.

When this surprising sight met the brethren's gaze,
the donkey pacing in the front, the lion, in like fashion,
marching in the rear, and the laden beasts in the middle,
they slipped quietly away to inform the blessed Jerome.
He came out and kindly bade them to set open the monastery gate.

"Take their loads off these our guests," said he, "the
camels, I mean, and the donkey, and bathe their feet and
give them food, and wait to see what God is minded to
show His servants."

Then, when all instructions as to the camels had been
obeyed, began the lion as of old to go here and there in

high feather through the cloister, flattening himself at the feet of each brother and wagging his tail, as though to ask forgiveness for the crime that he had never committed. Whereupon the brethren, full of shame for the cruel charge they had brought against him, would say to one another, "Behold our trusty shepherd whom so short a while ago we were upbraiding for a greedy ruffian. Now God has sent him to us with such a miracle to clear his character!"

Meantime the blessed Jerome, aware of things to come, spoke to the brethren, saying, "Be prepared, my brethren, in all things that are needed for refreshment; so that those who are about to be our guests may be received, as is fitting, without embarrassment."

His orders duly obeyed, the brethren were chatting with the blessed Jerome, when suddenly a messenger came with the news that there were guests at the gate. At this Jerome commanded that the doors of the monastery be opened and the visitors brought to him.

The merchants came in, blushing, and cast themselves at the feet of the blessed man, begging forgiveness. Gently raising them up, he told them to enjoy their own goods with thanksgiving, but not to take the goods of others. This marvelous pardon ended, he bade them accept refreshment and take again their camels and go their way.

Then with one voice they cried out, "We beg you, Father, that you will accept, for the lamps in the church and the need of the brethren, half of the oil that the camels have brought. For we are sure that it was rather to be of service to you than for our own profit that we went down into Egypt to bargain there."

To which the blessed Jerome replied, "This that you ask is indeed not right, for it would seem a great hardship that we who ought to have pity on others and relieve their needs by our own giving, should bear so heavy on you, taking your property away from you when we are not in need of it."

To which they answered, "Neither this food, nor any of our own property do we touch, unless you first command that what we ask shall be done. Accept half of the oil that the camels have brought, and we pledge ourselves to give to you this measure of oil in each succeeding year."

So therefore, compelled by the violence of their entreaties, the blessed Jerome commanded that their prayer should be fulfilled. They took refreshment and, after receiving both benediction and camels, they returned to their own people. But that these things were done at Bethlehem, and the fashion of their doing, is confidently told among the inhabitants of that place until this day.

Juniper

EILEEN DUGGAN

Who does not love the juniper tree?
The scent of its branches comes back to me,
And ever I think of the Holy Three
Who came to rest by the juniper tree!
Joseph and Mary and little wee Son
Came to rest when the day was done!
And the little Child slept on His Mother's knee
In the shelter sweet of the juniper tree!

Gabriel

WILLARD WATTLES

Mary walked in the daisies
Along a winding way;
The wind came by and touched her,
Her face was glad and gay;
Something nestled in her heart,
The sad Christ smiled that day.

Mary bore the daisies
Home in her two hands,
Daisies of white petals
For all the lonely lands,
That will not fade or vanish
While the arch of Heaven stands.

A Song

JOHN HENRY NEWMAN

The holy Monks, concealed from man,
In midnight choir, or studious cell,
In sultry field, or wintry glen,
The holy Monks, I love them well.

The Friars too, the zealous band
By Dominic or Francis led,
They gather, and they take their stand
Where foes are fierce, or friends have fled.

O holy Monks and Friars dear,
Look on these little ones, that we
Thy saintliness may copy here,
And in the eternal Kingdom see.

Of the many legends told about beloved Saint Nicholas,
none is more amusing than

Ill-Luck and the Fiddler

HOWARD PYLE

Once upon a time Saint Nicholas came down into the
world to take a peep at the old place and see how things
looked in the springtime. On he stepped along the road
to the town where he used to live, for he had a notion
to find out whether things were going on nowadays as
they one time did. By and by he came to a crossroad,
and whom should he see sitting there but Ill-Luck himself! Ill-Luck's face was as gray as ashes, and his hair as
white as snow, for he is as old as Grandfather Adam;
and two great wings grew out of his shoulders, for he
flies fast and comes quickly to those whom he visits,
does Ill-Luck.

Now Saint Nicholas had a pocketful of hazelnuts,
which he kept cracking and eating as he trudged along
the road, and just then he came upon one with a worm-
hole in it. When he saw Ill-Luck it came into his head to
do a good turn to poor mankind.

"Good morning, Ill-Luck," says he.

"Good morning, Saint Nicholas," says Ill-Luck.

"You look as hale and strong as ever," says Saint
Nicholas.

"Ah, yes," says Ill-Luck, "I find plenty to do."

"They tell me," says Saint Nicholas, "that you can
go wherever you choose, even if it be through a keyhole;
now, is that so?"

"Yes," says Ill-Luck, "it is."

"Well, look now, friend," says Saint Nicholas, "could you go into this hazelnut if you chose to?"

"Yes," says Ill-Luck, "I could indeed."

"I should like to see you," says Saint Nicholas, "for then I should be of a mind to believe what people say of you."

"Well," says Ill-Luck, "I have not much time to be pottering and playing upon Jack's fiddle, but to oblige an old friend"—thereupon he made himself small and smaller, and phst! he was in the nut in a wink.

Then what do you think Saint Nicholas did? In his hand he held a little plug of wood, and no sooner had Ill-Luck entered the nut than he stuck the plug in the hole, and there was man's enemy as tight as a fly in a bottle.

"So!" says Saint Nicholas, "that's a piece of work well done." Then he tossed the hazelnut under the roots of an oak tree close by and went his way.

And that is how this story begins.

Well, the hazelnut lay and lay and lay, and all the time that it lay there nobody met with ill luck; but one day who should come traveling that way but a rogue of a Fiddler, with his fiddle under his arm. The day was warm, and he was tired, so down he sat under the shade of the oak tree to rest his legs. By and by he heard a little shrill voice piping and crying, "Let me out! let me out! let me out!"

The Fiddler looked up and down, but he could see nobody. "Who are you?" says he.

"I am Ill-Luck! Let me out! let me out!"

"Let you out?" says the Fiddler. "Not I. If you are bottled up here, it is the better for all of us." And so saying, he tucked his fiddle under his arm and off he marched.

But before he had gone six steps he stopped. He was one of your peering, prying sort, and liked more than a little to know all that was to be known about this or that or the other thing that he chanced to see or hear. "I wonder where Ill-Luck can be, to be in such a tight place as he seems to be caught in," says he to himself, and back he came again. "Where are you, Ill-Luck?" says he.

"Here I am," says Ill-Luck, "here in this hazelnut, under the roots of the oak tree."

Thereupon the Fiddler laid aside his fiddle and bow, and fell to poking and prying under the roots until he found the nut. Then he began twisting and turning it in his fingers, looking first on one side and then on the other, and all the while Ill-Luck kept crying, "Let me out! let me out!"

It was not long before the Fiddler found the little

56

wooden plug, and then nothing would do but he must take a peep inside the nut to see if Ill-Luck was really there. So he picked and pulled at the wooden plug until at last out it came. And phst! pop! out came Ill-Luck along with it.

Plague take the Fiddler! say I.

"Listen," says Ill-Luck. "It has been many a long day that I have been in that hazelnut, and you are the man that has let me out. For once in a way I will do a good turn to a poor human body."

Therewith, and without giving the Fiddler time to speak a word, Ill-Luck caught him up by the belt, and whiz! away he flew like a bullet over hill and over valley, over moor and over mountain, so fast that not enough wind was left in the Fiddler's lungs to say "Boo!"

By and by he came to a garden, and there he let the Fiddler drop on the soft grass below. Then away he flew to attend to other matters of greater need.

When the Fiddler had gathered his wits together and himself to his feet, he saw that he lay in a beautiful garden of flowers and fruit trees and marble walks and what not; and that at the end of it stood a great, splendid house, all built of white marble, with a fountain in front, and peacocks strutting about on the lawn.

Well, the Fiddler smoothed down his hair and brushed his clothes a bit, and off he went to see what was to be seen in the grand house at the end of the garden.

He entered the door, and nobody said no to him. Then he passed through one room after another, and each was finer than the other. Many servants stood around, but they only bowed, and never asked whence he came.

At last he came to a room where a little old man sat at a table. The table was spread with a feast that smelled so good that it brought tears to the Fiddler's eyes and water to his mouth, and all the plates were of pure gold. The little old man sat alone, but another place was spread, as though he were expecting someone. As the Fiddler came in the little old man nodded and smiled. "Welcome!" he cried; "and have you come at last?"

"Yes," answered the Fiddler, "I have. It was Ill-Luck that brought me."

"Nay," said the little old man, "do not say that. Sit down to the table and eat; and when I have told you all, you will say it was not Ill-Luck, but Good-Luck, that brought you."

The Fiddler had his own mind about that; but, all the same, down he sat at the table and fell to with knife and fork at the good things, as though he had not had a bit to eat for a week of Sundays.

"I am the richest man in the world," said the little old man after a while.

"I am glad to hear it," replied the Fiddler.

"You may well be," said the old man, "for I am all alone in the world, and without wife or child. And this morning I said to myself that the first body that came to my house I would take for a son or a daughter, as the case might be. You are the first, and so you shall live with me as long as I live, and after I am gone everything that I have shall be yours."

The Fiddler did nothing but stare with open eyes and mouth, as though he would never shut either again.

Well, the Fiddler lived with the old man for maybe three or four days as snug and happy a life as ever a mouse passed in a green cheese. As for the gold and silver and jewels, why, they were as plentiful in that house as dust in a mill! Everything the Fiddler wanted came to his hand. He lived high, and slept soft and warm, and never knew what it was to want either more or less, or great or small. In all those three or four days he did nothing but enjoy himself with might and main.

But by and by he began to wonder where all the good things came from. Then, before long, he fell to pestering the old man with questions about the matter.

At first the old man put him off with short answers, but the Fiddler was a master hand at finding out anything that he wanted to know. He dinned and drummed and worried until flesh and blood could stand it no longer. So at last the old man said that he would show him the treasure house, and at that the Fiddler was pleased beyond measure.

The old man took a key from behind the door and led him out into the garden. There in a corner by the wall was a great trapdoor of iron. The old man fitted the key to the lock and turned it. He lifted the door, and then went down a steep flight of stone steps, and the Fiddler followed close at his heels. Down below it was as light as day, for in the center of the room hung a great lamp that shone with a bright light and lighted up all the place. On the floor were set three great basins of marble: one was nearly full of silver, one of gold, and one of gems of all sorts.

"All this is mine," said the old man, "and after I am gone it shall be yours. It was left to me as I shall leave it to you; and in the meantime you may come and go as you choose and fill your pockets whenever you wish to. But there is one thing you must not do: you must never open that door yonder at the back of the room. Should you do so, Ill-Luck will be sure to overtake you."

Oh, no! the Fiddler would never think of doing such a thing as opening the door. The silver and gold and jewels were enough for him. But since the old man had given him permission, he would just help himself to a few of the fine things. So he stuffed his pockets full, and then he followed the old man up the steps and out into the sunlight again.

It took him maybe an hour to count all the money and jewels he had brought up with him. After he had done that, he began to wonder what was inside the little door at the back of the room. First he wondered; then he began to grow curious; then he began to itch and tingle and burn as though fifty thousand I-want-to-know nettles were sticking into him from top to toe. At last he could stand it no longer. "I'll just go down yonder," said he, "and peep through the keyhole; perhaps I can see what is there without opening the door."

So down he took the key, and off he marched to the garden. He opened the trapdoor and went down the steep steps to the room below. There was the door at the end of the room; but when he came to look, there was no keyhole to it. "Pshaw!" said he, "here is a pretty state of affairs. Tut! tut! tut! Well, since I have come so far, it would be a pity to turn back without seeing more." So he opened the door and peeped in.

"Pooh!" said the Fiddler, "there's nothing there, after all," and he opened the door wide.

Before him was a great long passageway, and at the far end of it he could see a spark of light as though the sun were shining there. He listened, and after a while he heard a sound like the waves beating on the shore. "Well," says he, "this is the most curious thing I have seen for a long time. Since I have come so far, I may as well see the end of it." So he entered the passageway and closed the door behind him.

He went on and on, and the spark of light kept growing larger and larger, and by and by, pop! out he came at the other end of the passage.

Sure enough, there he stood on the seashore, with the waves beating and dashing on the rocks. He stood looking and wondering to find himself in such a place, when all of a sudden something came with a whiz and a rush and caught him by the belt, and away he flew like a bullet.

By and by he managed to screw his head around and look up, and there it was Ill-Luck that had him. "I thought so," said the Fiddler, and then he gave over kicking.

Well, on and on they flew, over hill and valley, over moor and mountain, until they came to another garden, and there Ill-Luck let the Fiddler drop.

Swash! down he fell into the top of an apple tree, and there he hung in the branches.

It was the garden of a royal castle, and all had been weeping and woe (though they were beginning now to pick up their smiles again), and this was the reason why— the king of that country had died, and no one was left behind him but the queen. But she was a prize, for not only was the kingdom hers, but she was as young as a spring apple and as pretty as a picture, so that there was no end of those who would have liked to have her, each man for his own. Even that day there were three princes at the castle, each one wanting the queen to marry him; and the wrangling and bickering and squabbling that was going on was enough to deafen a body. The poor young queen was tired to death with it all, and so she had come out into the garden for a bit of rest; and there she sat under the shade of an apple tree, fanning herself and crying, when—

Swash! down fell the Fiddler into the apple tree, and down fell a dozen apples, popping and tumbling about the queen's ears.

The queen looked up and screamed, and the Fiddler climbed down.

"Where did you come from?" said she.

"Oh, Ill-Luck brought me," said the Fiddler.

"Nay," said the queen, "do not say so. You fell from heaven, for I saw it with my eyes and heard it with my ears. I see how it is now. You were sent hither from heaven to be my husband, and my husband you shall be. You shall be king of this country, half and half with me as queen, and shall sit on a throne beside me."

You can guess whether or not that was music to the Fiddler's ears.

So the princes were sent packing, and the Fiddler was married to the queen and reigned in that country.

Well, three or four days passed, and all was as sweet and happy as a spring day. But at the end of that time the Fiddler began to wonder what was to be seen in the castle. The queen was very fond of him and was glad enough to show him all the fine things there were; so hand in hand they went everywhere, from garret to cellar.

But you should have seen how splendid it all was! The Fiddler felt more certain than ever that it was better to be a king than to be the richest man in the world, and he was as glad as glad can be that Ill-Luck had brought him from the rich little old man over yonder to this.

So he saw everything in the castle but one thing. "What is behind that door?" said he.

"Ah! that," said the queen, "you must not ask or wish to know. Should you open that door, Ill-Luck will be sure to overtake you."

"Pooh!" said the Fiddler, "I don't care to know, anyhow," and off they went, hand in hand.

Yes, that was a very fine thing to say; but before an hour had gone by, the Fiddler's head began to hum and buzz like a beehive. "I don't believe," said he, "there would be a grain of harm in my peeping inside that door; all the same, I will not do it. I will just go down and peep through the keyhole."

So off he went to do as he said, but there was no keyhole to that door either. "Why, look!" said he, "it is just like the door at the rich man's house over yonder; I wonder if it is the same inside as outside," and he opened the door and peeped in. Yes; there was the long passage and the spark of light at the far end, as though the sun were shining. He cocked his head to one side and listened. "Yes," said he, "I think I hear the water rushing, but I am not sure; I will just go a little farther in and listen," and so he entered and closed the door behind him. Well, he went on and on until, pop! there he was out at the farther end, and before he knew what he was about he had stepped out upon the seashore, just as he had done before.

Whiz! whir! away flew the Fiddler like a bullet, and there was Ill-Luck carrying him by the belt again. Away they sped, over hill and valley, over moor and mountain, until the Fiddler's head grew so dizzy that he had to shut his eyes. Suddenly Ill-Luck let him drop, and down he fell, thump! bump! on the hard ground. Then he opened his eyes and sat up, and lo and behold! there he was under the oak tree whence he had started in the first place. There lay his fiddle, just as he had left it. He picked it up and ran his fingers over the strings, trum, twang! Then he got to his feet and brushed the dirt and grass from his knees. He tucked his fiddle under his arm, and off he stepped upon the way he had been going at first.

"Just to think!" said he, "I should either have been the richest man in the world, or else I should have been a king, if it had not been for Ill-Luck."

And that is the way we all of us talk.

Ring Out, Wild Bells

ALFRED, LORD TENNYSON

[Choir to be arranged in three voices: high, medium, and low]

High   Ring out, wild bells, to the wild sky,
Medium   The flying cloud, [Medium, high] the frosty light;
Low   The year is dying in the night;
All   Ring out, wild bells, and let him die.

Low   Ring out the old, [High] ring in the new,
Medium, high   Ring, happy bells, across the snow;
Low   The year is going, let him go;
Medium, low   Ring out the false, [All] ring in the true.

Low   Ring out a slowly dying cause,
And ancient forms of party strife;
Medium   Ring in the nobler modes of life,
Medium, high   With sweeter manners, purer laws.

Low   Ring out the want, the care, the sin,
The faithless coldness of the times;
Medium   Ring out, ring out my mournful rhymes,
Medium, high   But ring the fuller minstrel in.

Low   Ring out false pride in place and blood,
Medium   The civic slander and the spite;
High, medium   Ring in the love of truth and right,
All   Ring in the common love of good.

Medium, high   Ring in the valiant man and free,
The larger heart, the kindlier hand;
Low   Ring out the darkness of the land,
All   Ring in the Christ that is to be.

The Seven Sleepers

PADRAIC COLUM

The roots of the cedars of Lebanon[1] grew down into that cavern, and in their tangles a thousand bats huddled together. Every seven years the dog that was Malchus's[2] dog wakened up. Raising his head he would see his master and his master's six friends lying, one beside the other, fast asleep.

The dog that was Malchus's dog would smell around, but nothing would come to him except the smell that he had known in burrows—the smell of dry earth. There would be no stir in the air around him; there would be no movement upon the ground; there would be no daylight. The thousand bats, high above him, made no sound and gave no stir. With his head raised, the dog that was Malchus's dog would look at his master, expecting that his voice would come to him. No voice would come, and the dog would turn round and sleep again.

Every seven years for fifty times seven years the dog would wake up; still his master and his master's six friends lay there. Then, one day, light streamed into the cavern, for the stones that had been set at its mouth were removed. The dog waked up. Seeing the daylight, the dog barked. Malchus, his master, waked up. And then the other six sleepers awakened.

They awakened and they said to one another, "We have slept; even through the hours of our great danger we slept." They saw daylight streaming in and each

1. *cedars of Lebanon* (lĕb'à nŏn): evergreen trees that attain great age. 2. *Malchus's* (măl'kŭs's).

said, "It is not as we thought it was." Each thought that he had dreamed of the cavern being closed upon them by their persecutors with immovable stones.

For these youths had been persecuted by Decius,[3] consul of the Romans, who had dominion over seventy-two kings. The consul had been moved to persecute the Christians of the city of Ephesus.[4] He had a proclamation made, saying that all who would not go into the pagan temples and make sacrifice to the pagan idols should be cut to pieces by his soldiers; he himself rode into the city to see that his command was carried out.

Nearly all who were in the city forsook the Christian faith. But there were seven youths who would not forsake it, nor go into the pagan temples and make sacrifice to the pagan idols. These seven were friends who were devoted to one another, and their names were Malchus, Marcian,[5] Dionysius,[6] John, Serapion,[7] Maximian,[8] and Constantine.

They stole from the city, and they went towards the mountain, and the dog that was Malchus's dog followed them. They hid within a cavern. Then one went back to the city to buy food. The shopkeeper who sold him meal made a little hole in the bag so that the meal trickled out, leaving a track where he went. And the consul, mounted on his horse, followed this track and came to the cavern where the seven had hidden themselves. He signed to his followers, and they drew heavy stones and closed up the entrance of the cavern.

"In a while," the consul said, "none will be left

3. *Decius* (dē'sĭ ŭs).   4. *Ephesus* (ĕf'ĕ sŭs): an ancient city in Asia Minor.
5. *Marcian* (mär'shĭ ăn).   6. *Dionysius* (dī'ŏ nĭsh'ĭ ŭs).   7. *Serapion* (sĕ rā'pĭ ŏn).
8. *Maximian* (măx ĭm'ĭ ăn).

alive in Ephesus or around it who have the Christian faith." And the consul rejoiced as he said this.

The seven in the cavern sat together; they saw the daylight being shut out, and they knew from the scornful shouts of those outside that they had been shut in so that they never could leave the cavern. They sat there talking to one another, and weeping and consoling one another. Then they slept. The dog that was Malchus's dog crept close to them, and he, too, slept, but every seven years he awakened.

And after a hundred years, and another hundred, and a third hundred years had passed, a man came to the side of that mountain, and seeking weighty stones for

the building of a roadway, took away the stones that were at the mouth of the cavern. It was then that the daylight streamed in on where they lay. It was then that the dog that was Malchus's dog barked. It was then that they awakened—Malchus, Marcian, Dionysius, John, Serapion, Maximian, and Constantine. It was then that each said, "It is not as I thought; the mouth of the cavern is not closed upon us."

They were hungry. Malchus told his friends that he would steal into the city and buy bread. They let him go, and he went out of the cavern, and down the side of the mountain, and along the road that went to the city of Ephesus. When he came before the gate of the city he was astonished. For behold! over the gate of the city was the cross of the Christian faith. He thought that this could be nothing but a trick to bring back to the city the Christians who had fled from it. And in greater fear than ever he went through the gate and into the city.

He had lived in a wide street in that city, but now he went down byways so that he might not be met by those who knew him. He came to a baker's shop that was away from the main part of the town, and he went within. He saluted the baker, and the baker returned his salutation in the name of Christ. Malchus was fearful, thinking that the words were said to trap him, but he pretended not to have heard what the baker said. He took the loaves from him and handed him a silver coin in payment.

When the baker received the coin, he looked at Malchus sharply. He then went to the back of the shop and spoke to some who were there. Malchus was about to steal out of the shop when the baker came and laid hands on him, saying, "Nay, you must not go until you have told us where the treasure is that you found."

"I found no treasure," Malchus said to him.

"Where, then, did you get the ancient coin that you have given me in payment for the loaves? Assuredly you have found a treasure."

When the baker said this to him, Malchus gave himself up for lost, for he thought that this talk about treasure was but a pretence to hold him until they examined him on the charge of being a Christian.

The men in the baker's shop laid hold on Malchus, and they put a rope around his neck, and they dragged him into the market place. They said to those who crowded around, "Here is one who has found a treasure that must be given to the consul, and we would have a reward for making him reveal where that treasure now is."

Malchus, in the market place, looked all round him. He saw no one there whom he knew, and he could see that no one in the crowd knew him. He said to those who were around, "Tell me, I implore you, what city is this that I have come into?"

They said, "You are playing the madman, pretending that you do not know that this is the great city of Ephesus."

It was then that Malchus saw coming through the crowd one in the robes of a Christian bishop.

"Who is the youth, and why is he being treated by the Ephesians in this way?" he asked.

And Malchus heard those around him say, "He has offered a coin of the reign of an ancient consul in payment for loaves of bread, and he dares to say that it is of the money that his parents gave him. Assuredly he has found a treasure, but he will tell none of the Ephesians where the treasure now is."

Malchus saw that the one who came to him was indeed a bishop, and he was more and more bewildered. The bishop came and spoke tenderly to him. Then said Malchus, "I implore you to tell me where the consul Decius has gone to."

The bishop said, "Decius is not our consul's name. There has not been a consul of the name of Decius for three hundred years." And then he said, "If, as you say, you have parents and friends living in the city of Ephesus, tell us their names, so that we may bring them to you."

Then Malchus gave the names of his parents and the names of the friends he knew in Ephesus. No one in the crowd had heard of them. The bishop then told him that he might go to the place where he thought his parents lived. Malchus went there, the bishop and the people following him. And when he came to the place where his parents' house had stood, behold! what he saw there was a pool of water with birds dipping their wings in it.

When he saw this, he wept. Then to the bishop and those who were with the bishop he said, "I do not understand what I look upon. I thought that I was in great danger in coming here, thinking that it was only yesterday that the Christians of Ephesus were being put to the sword. But I see the cross surmounting the churches, and I see the Christian bishop having authority. And yet it is to me as if I had come into a city of the dead.

Let me, I pray you, go back to the cavern where I left my companions."

The bishop signed to those who were guarding him, and they let Malchus go. He went, and they followed him towards the mountain. He entered the cavern. He saw his six friends, Marcian, Dionysius, John, Serapion, Maximian, and Constantine, and they welcomed him joyfully. He gave them the bread he had brought, and they ate, and were happy. But when they asked of him what signs he saw of the persecution of Christians in Ephesus, he wept. And then he told them that all they had known in Ephesus had passed away, the good with the evil, and that there was no persecution of Christians there, and that the cross was reared in triumph over the churches and that their parents and all whom they knew were dead and long passed away.

His friends listened to him in wonder. And while he was still speaking, the bishop came into the cavern.

"Bless us, Holiness," the seven youths said to him.

"Nay, it is you should bless me and bless the people

of Ephesus," the bishop said, "seeing that it was on you that God bestowed the most signal favor—the favor of keeping you in life to witness the triumph of the cross in Ephesus and in the whole of the east of the world." Then the bishop led them without, and the seven stood on the side of the mountain and blessed the people who came that way on the morning of Easter, carrying the cross.

As they stood there, it seemed to the seven of them— to Malchus, Marcian, Dionysius, John, Serapion, Maximian, and Constantine—that every clod within was making melody, such music came to them from the cavern. Again they went within. Then they lay down as before, and the dog that was Malchus's dog lay near them. And lying there their souls went from them, and they passed out of this life. And, behold! a rose tree grew up where they had lain, and its branches spread out and grew over the mouth of the cavern, wreathing it in roses.

A Street in Nazareth

GERALD M. C. FITZGERALD, C.S.C.

There is a street in Nazareth,
  Hard white beneath sun glare,
But soft and gray at eventide
  When townfolk gather there;
And we know all its foot-worn stones
  And travel them in prayer.
We watch the street of Nazareth
  Where Christ and Mary part,
And though we dwell long leagues away,
  That street runs through our heart.

The Splendid Cause

PATRICK O'CONNOR, S.S.C.

Who has a blade for a splendid cause
  Who has a heart that's true,
To live and fight for the grandest thing
That man could dream, or singer sing,
  Or ever soldier knew?

Who would go forth on toilsome ways
  By saints and heroes trod,
And join with a gallant company
In a glorious, deathless chivalry—
  The Chivalry of God?

For this is the dream that the old men dreamt,
  The vision the young men see—
To march in the glory of Pentecost,
To bear to the nations the sweet white Host
  And the truth to make them free.

Then let not the knightly slogan die,
  Nor the knightly weapons fall,
Till every land is His Holy Land,
Where His lamp is lit and His altars stand
  And His Cross is over all.

So flash out your blades for the splendid cause
  And pray that your hearts be true,
To live and fight for the grandest thing
That man could dream, or singer sing,
  Or ever soldier knew!

Hail and Farewell

ABRAM J. RYAN

The New Year kneels low in the starry sky
 And asks the Old
To bless us all with love, and life, and light,
 And joy untold.

The Old Year marches on its way.
 We look, and lo!
The past is passing, and the present seems
 To wish to go.

The olden golden stories of the brave,
 That stirred the earth,
Shall never die but, in the future years,
 Find bright re-birth.

The pageantry that thrilled each passing age
 With deeds of men,
Is set down in the golden Book of Life
 With deathless pen.

The Old Year dies! With song and ringing bell
 It drives out care;
The New Year spans the threshold of the Lord
 With solemn prayer.

By the Mediterranean Shores

All Christian nations claim spiritual ancestry from the men and women who served the Son of God.

Italy claims Peter and Paul, those valiant men of God who crossed the wide blue waters of the Mediterranean Sea to spread the simple gospel of the humble Christ who died upon the Cross.

Spain boasts that James, son of the fisherman Zebedee of Galilee, preached Christianity there and is buried in the great Spanish shrine of Compostela.

France glories in tracing its Christian origin to the sorrowing family of Martha and Lazarus and Mary Magdalene, who made miraculous journey across the Mediterranean from Judea to the south of France.

Out of the faith of the disciples of Christ came the message of the Catholic Church to the lands along the Mediterranean. Out of the Catholic Church came the literature of these lands. For great Christian writers not only saved the worthy writings of the past; they also created a great new literature of their own.

The Mediterranean has witnessed the great drama of the world. Bargemen, longshoremen, sailmakers, sailors along its shores heard the tramp of Roman legions. They saw the torches of pagan emperors blaze in the soft Mediterranean nights. They beheld Christians mobbed, stoned, blinded by blood. But they also heard the trumpet words of Peter, who preached the Word of Christ, and of Paul, who shouted the exultant story of his conversion. This great conflict of Christianity is the source of some of the world's great literature.

South of the city of Naples is Mount Vesuvius. On a day
of bright August sunlight, seventy-nine years after the birth
of Christ, the great crater erupted and buried
the neighboring town of Pompeii. It had been a place
of ancient houses and stately temples, of theaters and forums,
and of wide streets where merchants sold their wares, but,
in a sudden rain of volcanic ash, a civilization perished.
Centuries later scientists dug through the ruins
and reclaimed Pompeii. Today in the land where Peter
was crucified that men might learn the eternal truth of Christ,
men and women make pilgrimage to a shrine to His Mother.
There they kneel and say

Prayer of the Pilgrims at Pompeii

O Queen of the Rosary, in these days of dead faith and triumphant impiety, thou hast been pleased to establish thy throne as Queen and Mother in the ancient land of Pompeii, once the home of paganism. From this place, where men of old worshipped idols and evil spirits, do thou this day, as the Mother of divine graces, scatter far and wide the treasures of heaven's mercy.

Drifting

THOMAS BUCHANAN READ

Choir to be arranged in three voices: high, medium, and low.]

My soul today
Is far away,
Sailing the Vesuvian Bay;
My wingèd boat,
A bird afloat,
Swings round the purple peaks remote:—

Round purple peaks
It sails, and seeks
Blue inlets and their crystal creeks,
Where high rocks throw,
Through deeps below,
A duplicated golden glow.

Far, vague, and dim,
The mountains swim;
While on Vesuvius' misty brim,
With outstretched hands,
The gray smoke stands
O'erlooking the volcanic lands.

I heed not, if
My rippling skiff
Float swift or slow from cliff to cliff;
With dreamful eyes
My spirit lies
Under the walls of Paradise.

The Christian Slave

In a sunny valley, deep among the seven hills of Rome, Fabiola[1] lived in the house of her father. In all of Rome there was no house more splendid. In all of Rome there was no lady more beautiful.

The emperor in his palace on the Quirinal[2] said that Fabiola was lovely, and every young and noble Roman paid court because of her beauty and her wealth. They came from the great palaces of Rome to the house that Fabius had built for his only child.

"Where will you find such carpets?" murmured the Romans as they passed beneath the porticos and beyond the third large court. "Or such silks?" "Or such ivories?"

For out of Babylon and China and of India and of all the lands beyond had come the hangings and the lamps and the ornaments that filled the marble hallways and lined the marble stairway.

"Where will you find such beauty?" sighed the young nobles as they looked upon Fabiola.

Three slave girls of the house of Fabius heard them. "Where *will* you find such beauty?" whispered Afra, who had been brought out of a darker continent to serve Fabiola.

"Where, indeed?" softly answered Graia[3] the Greek.

Only Syra, slim and dark and young, said nothing. Silently she thrust her shining needle into the soft embroidery of a silken robe for the loveliest of Romans, but she could remember a deeper beauty in a far-off land where Christ had once walked His quiet way and where

1. *Fabiola* (fà bē′ô là). one of the seven hills of Rome.
2. *Quirinal* (kwĭr′ĭ năl): site of the government on
3. *Graia* (grā′yà).

81

men had openly proclaimed Him. Syra had known beauty in the new prayers of the Christians, in flickering candlelight, in the lifted hand of a priest at an altar beneath the purple cedars of Lebanon, in hymns of praise to One Who had died that men might be free. This had been before she had been brought as a slave to Rome and, with the carpets and the silks and the hangings upon the walls of the house of Fabius, had been given to his daughter.

At first Fabiola did not seem to notice the girl's silence. "She has so much flattery," thought Syra, "that she will not miss praise from me."

One evening, though, as the sun dropped low over the

hills and the house and over the terrace where the fountain glistened, the silence of the slave girl crept like a shadow into the glass-walled room where Fabiola rested.

Fabiola stirred upon her silver couch. "Afra! Graia! Syra!" she summoned them and, when they stood beside her, said, "I have a silver mirror. Bring it to me!"

Afra handed her the shining mirror with its long handle of precious jewels.

Fabiola looked into its shimmering depths. "When I dine in my father's hall tonight all women must envy me," she said.

Afra held up an ivory jar of ointment as soft and as white as the swans in the blue waters of the garden pond. "This is the secret of beauty," she said. "I learned it in my own land where I learned, too, of magic charms and poisons."

The Greek slave shook out a gown of cloth of gold. "This is the secret of beauty," she said. "It cost me many trials before I could make anything so perfect."

Syra stood silently and said nothing.

"How delighted I should be, most noble creature," said Afra, and her voice was as smooth as the cream she was spreading across the glowing cheeks of Fabiola, "if I could see you as you entered your father's hall tonight."

The Greek girl folded a shining pleat into the gown of gold. "I should not presume to aspire to so high an honor as even to carry your draperies which will float from this robe like golden wings," she said.

Syra, slim and dark against the sunset, said nothing.

Then she saw Fabiola looking at her. "I have a golden

83

stiletto," said Fabiola, and her eyes did not leave Syra's face as she gave command, "Bring it to me!"

"Oh, no!" cried Afra.

"Mercy, noble mistress," cried the Greek, for this was the weapon with which Roman ladies punished their slaves.

"Bring it to me, Syra!"

Syra lifted the sharp-pointed knife from a richly carved table and placed it in Fabiola's hand.

"Now tell me," said Fabiola, and her face was as cruel as the stiletto that she held, "what would you desire?"

Syra smiled a little. "I have nothing to desire, noble lady," she said, "but that you may ever be happy."

Fabiola arose and faced her. "My happiness is easily attained," she said, and her eyes were bright with anger. "Methinks, slave, that you are not overgiven to praise. One seldom hears a soft word from you."

Syra lifted her head. "And what worth would flattery be from me?" she asked. "You hear it all day long from noble lips. Do you believe it when you hear it from *them*? Would you not despise it if you received it from *me*?"

Fabiola twisted the stiletto. "Have you yet to learn, Syra," she said, and rage clouded her voice, "that you are mine, and have been bought for me by my father at a high price, and that you must serve me as I please?"

Syra's dark eyes did not waver beneath the Roman's wrath. She did not speak.

"Do you know that I have as much right to your praise as I have to the work of your needle?" Fabiola's voice rose. "If it pleases me to be praised and flattered by you, do it you shall, whether you like it or not!"

"It is true," Syra answered, and her eyes were filled with tears, "that my life belongs to you, and so does all else that ends with life. All this you have bought with your gold, and it is yours just as are the gardens and the fountains and the chests of jewels and the wealth of Rome and—"

"Then how dare you—"

Now the tears were gone from Syra's eyes. "I dare," she said, and her head was high, "for I hold as my own something no emperor can purchase, no chains of slavery fetter, no limit of life contain."

The stiletto was nearer. "And, pray, what is that?"

Syra did not move. "It is a soul!" she said.

"A soul!" Fabiola's eyes flashed with fury. "Let me ask you what you mean by the word?"

"I only know," Syra answered her, "that a soul is an unseen gift from God that lives within me. Because of it I seek truth and honor in this life and glory forever in the world to come."

Afra and Graia stood apart in stricken fear. Then, with swift impatience, Fabiola spoke again. "Where did you learn all this folly? Do you, an ignorant, uneducated slave, pretend to know more than I? Or do you really believe that after death, when you will be thrown upon a heap of slaves and buried in a common pit, you will survive and know joy and freedom?"

"I shall survive!" said Syra, and it was as though golden chimes rang out and silver trumpets answered them. "I shall know freedom! I shall know joy everlasting!"

"What wild visions of an Eastern fancy are these?" Fabiola's rage filled the darkening room. "In what school have you heard this nonsense? I never read of it in any Greek or Latin book."

"It is the creed of the Man of Galilee," Syra told her with pride as militant as marching Roman legions. "It is the creed that one day will belong to every land, for in it there is no barrier between Roman or barbarian, between freeman or slave."

Fabiola moved closer, and scorn lashed her words. "What!" she exclaimed, "without waiting even for that future ideal life after death, you even now presume to claim equality with me?"

"I do presume," said Syra.

"Perhaps you are superior to me?" Fabiola mocked her. "Come, tell me!"

Syra did not falter, for now, she knew, though death might come before a Roman dawn, she must speak of the

burning faith of the Christians. She must tell of martyrs who were giving up their lives for the Church that spread its glory even in the gloom of the catacombs. She must muster all the forces of her mind and heart and soul to pass on the blazing messages of Peter and of Paul, to spread the flaming word of the faith for which one Man had died upon a Cross. Now she faced Fabiola. "You are far superior to me in place, in power, in riches," she began, "but I—"

"Go on! Go on!" Fabiola cried.

"But even a slave whose hope is an immortal life," Syra said, and her voice grew deeper, for she spoke of the love that leads from darkness into light, "whose only emperor is the great God who rules the world, cannot hold herself inferior to one who lives for this life that will end at the grave."

With stricken pride that, for the first time in her pampered life, she had been rebuked, and by a slave girl, Fabiola turned in swift anger. Afra saw her lift her arm. Graia shielded her face against the blow. Syra waited as she watched the plunging passage of the knife toward her shoulder.

"A Christian!" cried Fabiola, as she thrust the stiletto deep into Syra's robe.

Blood flowed from the wound, but Syra did not cry out in pain, for she had known always that Christians must suffer that Christianity might live.

Then, suddenly overwhelmed by the cruelty of her act and ashamed of the anger that had caused it, Fabiola sobbed. "Go, go, and have the wound dressed at once!"

Syra moved toward the dark hallway.

"Wait!" Fabiola called after her. "Let me give you a ring to quiet my regret."

Syra took the glowing emerald that Fabiola drew from her blood-stained hand. She thought, as she turned away, that Fabiola would soon forget the day and the deed; she could not know then that she had sown the first seed of belief that one day would blossom into conversion of the proud, the beautiful Fabiola. She could not know that night that one day a Roman emperor would see in the heavens a bright cross with these letters of fire: *In this sign thou shalt conquer*, and that, in triumphant faith, he would call out from the dark catacombs into the golden sunlight of Rome the men and women of the army of God.

When alms were collected for the poor among the Christians who prayed in the hidden stillness of the church of Saint Pastor, among the offerings was a glowing emerald ring. The good priest Polycarp thought it must have been the gift of some very rich Roman lady; but He Who watched had seen it dropped into the chest by the bandaged arm of a slave girl whose eyes were as bright as the stars above the purple hills of her own far-away Lebanon.

Adapted from Fabiola by Cardinal Wiseman

Cornelia's Jewels

GEORGENE FAULKNER

Long, long ago, there lived in Rome a good mother named Cornelia. She was the daughter of the great Roman general Scipio.[1] Because he had conquered Africa, he was called "Africanus." Her husband was a great and good man named Tiberius Gracchus.[2] They had two sons and one daughter.

After her husband died, Cornelia lived for her children. She had Greek tutors to teach her boys in all the noble arts. As the boys heard the tales of the Greek heroes, they were anxious to do brave deeds. They felt that the greatest thing a man could do was to give his life for his country.

Their mother studied and read with them. She told them of their brave grandfather and of their noble father.

She said, "My sons, men now honor me because I am the daughter of the great general, Scipio Africanus. I trust that in time they will honor me for being the mother of the Gracchi."[3]

The boys, filled with her spirit of patriotism, answered, "Mother, we trust that at some time we, like our grandfather and our father, may be called upon to serve our country."

The elder son, Tiberius, was nine years older than his brother Caius.[4] To him his mother often said, "You are the elder and if you do that which is right, your younger

1. *Scipio Africanus* (sĭp'ĭ ō ăf rĭ kā'nŭs).   2. *Tiberius Gracchus* (tĭ bēr'ĭ ŭs grăk'ŭs).   3. *Gracchi* (grăk'kē): sons of the family of Gracchus.   4. *Caius* (kā'yŭs).

89

brother will choose the right also and follow in your footsteps."

At one time, the king of Egypt asked Cornelia to marry him, but she refused to be a queen and have great riches and wear a crown and costly robes and gems.

"No," she said, "my life belongs to my children. I would rather be a good mother than the wealthiest queen in all the land."

"Our mother looks like a queen," the young Caius said to his brother.

"Yes," answered Tiberius, "but our mother is greater than any queen in all the world, for she is always noble and kind."

One day a friend came to visit the mother. When the younger boy noted the gorgeous gown and jewels worn by the visitor, he said to his brother, "Our mother does

not wear rings on her fingers, or bracelets, or necklaces; she does not even wear a gold band in her hair, and look at her friend in all her glittering gems! Why does not our mother wear jewels, Tiberius?"

"Mother does not need to wear gems to make her more beautiful," answered the loyal son.

Then the mother sent for her sons who were permitted to dine with her and her friend out in the garden. After dinner, a servant brought a golden basket belonging to the friend, who opened it and showed them her gems. She had strings of priceless pearls, as white and fleecy as the clouds that floated overhead; sapphires, as blue as the summer skies; rubies, as red as the roses in their garden; while her opals glowed with many lights; and the diamonds sparkled in the sunlight.

"Oh, how beautiful, how wonderful!" gasped the two boys in delight.

Then the guest turned to Cornelia and said, "My friend, I see you wear no jewels, but surely you own gems that you will show me. Cornelia, where are your jewels?"

Then Cornelia drew her sons to her and, putting an arm about each, she threw back her head and said proudly, "These are my jewels."

The sons never forgot that scene in the garden.

"Our mother shall be proud of us," they said. "We shall be true to her teaching."

When they were men, they became great leaders in Rome.

The older brother, as he traveled about, saw that the poor people were oppressed by the rich. He tried to establish a law whereby the nobles would be obliged to give up some of their land and riches to these poor people. But the Romans were not ready to listen to this reformer. Tiberius laid down his life for the cause of liberty, for he was killed by a mob at the Temple of Jupiter.

A few years later his younger brother Caius tried, as he had always done, to follow in his brother's footsteps. He tried to carry out his brother's ideas, to right wrongs and give freedom and justice to the poor; but he also sacrificed his life for the people and was killed in a grove near Rome.

When the heartbroken mother heard that her younger son had been killed also, she said proudly, "The grandchildren of the great Scipio Africanus were my sons. They perished in the temple and groves of the gods, but they deserved to die in these holy spots, for they gave their lives for the noblest of ends—the happiness of the people."

When the people realized all that these leaders had tried to do for them, they placed a statue in Rome in honor of these two brothers. Later, when Cornelia died, the Roman citizens had her statue placed where all might see it, and on it were engraved the words:

Cornelia, the mother of the Gracchi.

Although this happened many years ago, we like to tell the story today, for we know that the most precious thing in all the world is mother love.

Mother and I in the May

MICHAEL EARLS, S. J.

Queens may ride in a gilded coach,
    With guards at every door;
Kings go out with their cavalry,
    Trumpeters playing before;
        And the city is gay in a royal way,
  Hail to the king! says the cannon's roar.

I am a king in my own good realm,
    And I have a royal sway;
Over the land is my mother Queen,
    All in a queenly way;
        And a throne have we, and chivalry,
Down in the valley of May.

For a Blind Beggar's Sign

CLEMENTE BIONDI

Translated from the Italian by Thomas Walsh

Take pity, signors, ye who pass me by,
　Where I am but an outcast on the street,
Lest it be said ye are more blind than I,
　That can refuse a brother bread to eat.

For on my brow God's hand hath laid a sign;
　Come, ye with sight—is not His meaning clear?—
"These eyes must virgin wait the Light Divine;
　Who sins, ye rich, if He stands starving here?"

Prayer to the Virgin

Translated by Gerard Sloyan

Lady, so high Thou art, so great Thy worth,
　that he in need of grace who seeks not Thee
　strips his desire of wings, though he would fly from
　earth.

Ah, such Thy kindness that not only he
　is helped who of Thee makes demand;
　but ofttimes, freely, dost Thou heed unspoken plea.

In Thee is mercy, in Thee sweet pity's outstretched hand,
　peace everlasting, and enshrined in Thee
　the sum of goodness for God's creatures planned.

Dante's *Paradiso*, Canto XXXIII, ll. 13–20

Franciscan Aspiration

VACHEL LINDSAY

Would I might wake Saint Francis in you all,
Brother of birds and trees, God's Troubadour,
Blinded with weeping for the sad and poor;
Our wealth undone, all strict Franciscan men,
Come, let us chant the canticle again
Of mother earth and the enduring sun.
God made each soul the lowly leper's slave;
God made us saints, and brave.

God's Troubadour

SOPHIE JEWETT

Assisi lies across the sea in beautiful Italy. It is a little city, built on a mountainside, with a great wall about it, and a castle on the height above. It looks very much as it did more than seven hundred years ago when Francis Bernardone,[1] son of Piero[2] Bernardone the merchant, lived there amidst its narrow crooked streets, its stone houses, its brown-tiled roofs, its blazing sunshine and bright color.

From his father Francis learned many strange and wonderful tales; stories of Charlemagne[3] and Roland[4]; of King Arthur and his Knights of the Round Table. From him he learned the merry songs of the wandering poets, troubadours, as they were called, who sang in the courts of kings and in the halls of nobles. Their songs were of

1. *Bernardone* (bär när dō′nå).   2. *Piero* (pyâ′rō).   3. *Charlemagne* (shär′lĕ mān): Charles the Great, King of the Franks and Emperor of the West. 4. *Roland* (rō′länd): the nephew of Charlemagne and a defender of the Christians.

95

brave knights in shining armor, and of ladies with white hands, beautiful eyes, and sweet, unforgettable names.

As Francis Bernardone grew from a boy to a man, he made friends with a company of youths, the sons of the greatest families of Assisi. Their fathers were counts, and dukes, and princes, and the lads were vain of the names they bore and of the palaces where they lived. It was a selfish company, bent on having a good time and thinking nothing of the comfort of other people.

The youths welcomed Francis into their fellowship because, though he had not a noble name, he had splendid clothes to wear and much money to spend; and because, among them all, no one laughed so merrily or sang so sweetly as the merchant's son. The hours always went more gaily when Francis was of the party, for it made one feel happy just to look at his bright face.

Piero Bernardone was proud that his son should be the friend of these young lords, but the lad's gentle mother grieved that her kindhearted little boy should grow to be a thoughtless man. Her heart ached in the night when the noisy group went laughing and shouting through the streets, and she could hear the voice of Francis, sweeter and louder than the rest, singing a bit of troubadour song that he had learned as a child:

> My heart is glad in springtime,
>   When April turns to May;
> When nightingales sing in the dark,
>   And thrushes sing by day.

The mother would listen till the laughter and singing were far away and faint, and the last sound was always the voice of her boy, which, indeed, she seemed to hear long after all was silent in the narrow street. When the neighbors complained that the noise of the boys was too bad to be endured, the merchant only laughed.

"It is the way of the world," he said. "Francis is no worse than the others."

But his wife would speak softly, with tears in her gentle eyes, "Wait, I have great hope that he will yet become a good Christian." The mother knew all that was best in the boy. She thought, "However careless he may be, he has a kind and loving heart." And she was right. In his happiest moments Francis was always quick to pity anyone who was poor or in pain.

But one who is thoughtless is always in danger of being cruel. One day a man, ragged and hungry, crept in at the

open door of Piero Bernardone's shop. Piero was absent, but Francis was spreading out beautiful silks and velvets before two customers, for he sometimes sold goods for his father. Standing in his dirty, brown rags among the red and purple stuffs and the gold embroideries, the beggar cried, "In the name of God, give me something, for I am starving!"

Francis, whose mind was intent on his bargain, impatiently sent the man away. A moment later, he was sorry. "What would I have done," he said to himself, "if that man had asked me for money in the name of a count or baron? What ought I to do when he comes in the name of God?" Leaving the astonished customers in the shop, the boy ran out into the street, found the beggar, and gave him all the money he had in his purse.

Despite his joy, Francis had times when he became thoughtful and was dissatisfied with himself. As he went up and down the streets of Assisi, well dressed and well fed, he saw people sick and hungry and ragged, glad to receive a crust of bread or an old cloak. "These people," thought Francis, "would live for months on the money that I waste in one day." Sometimes he would throw his purse to a starving man, or his bright cloak to a ragged one, and his merry friends would laugh at him for his folly. Then they would all ride away gaily, and even Francis would forget.

He did not forget his old love for the stories of King Arthur and the Round Table. He disliked more and more the thought of being a merchant. He wanted to travel, to see far-away countries, but he wanted to go as a soldier, not as a tradesman. He wanted to storm great castles, to rescue fair ladies, to ride at the head of a fearless band of knights. He loved the knights of the old stories, not alone because they were strong in battle, but because they were gracious in speech, true to their word, and kind to all the unfortunate and weak. Perhaps it was his love for gentle manners and brave deeds that kept Francis from becoming altogether hardhearted and selfish in these days.

Besides the songs of love and of battle, he had learned wise little verses about the duties of knighthood, and sometimes, when he and his friends had been most rude and unknightly, the old rhymes came back to his mind like a reproachful voice:

> Nowhere is such a noble name
>   As that of chivalry;
> Of coward acts and words of shame
>   It is the enemy;
> But wisdom, truth, valor in fight,
>   Pity and purity,
> These are the gifts that make a knight,
>   My friend, as you may see.

There were many and terrible wars in Italy in the thirteenth century, and the chance of trying his fortune as a soldier was not long in coming to Francis Bernardone.

Only fifteen miles away from Assisi stands a larger city, called Perugia.[5] It also is built upon a mountain, and the two towns seem to smile at each other across the green valley. But for hundreds of years there were only bitter looks and hatred between the two. Perugia, higher and stronger, lay like a dragon, ready to spring upon her small but furious enemy. Assisi, like a lion's cub, was

---

5. *Perugia* (på rōō′jä).

always ready to fight. Sometimes the lion was victor; always it was fierce enough to make the huge dragon writhe with pain.

When Francis Bernardone was about twenty years old, there was war between the great dragon and the little lion. Down from one mountain came the Perugian army. Down from the other came that of Assisi. With the army of Assisi rode Francis and most of the company of friends who had been so merry together in times of peace. They were happy as ever, and eager to see what a real battle might be like.

The armies met in the plain and fought by the river side, near a tiny town called the Bridge of St. John.

This time the Perugians were too strong for the Assisans, and the young soldier's first combat was a defeat. One day taught him all the horror of a field of battle. He saw men wounded and dying. He heard the terrified cries of riderless horses. He suffered from blinding sun and parching thirst. War, that he had thought so noble and glorious, seemed somehow confused and cruel and hideous.

The army of Assisi lost heavily that day. Many men were slain, many were made prisoners, and one of the prisoners was Francis Bernardone. He was too tired, too hungry, and too thirsty to feel anything keenly except the need of sleep and food; yet he wondered how it had all happened. Could he be the same man who had gone about for days delighting in the song of a warlike troubadour?

At last there came a day when the prisoners were set free, and Francis could return to his home. The wide valley, with its shining rivers, the far blue mountains, and the green forest must have been a welcome sight to eyes that, for a long year, had looked at the world through prison windows. But his young friends received him joyfully and the old life began once more.

When his friends began to tell him of the new fighting in the south of Italy and of a company of soldiers who were going from Assisi to join the army of a famous knight, the old love of battle and glory woke in his heart, and Francis made haste that he might be ready to go to war again.

His mother watched him with grave eyes as he rode away.

Francis and his fellow-soldiers were to spend the first night in Spoleto,[6] a city about twenty miles south of Assisi, on the way to Rome. The road ran along at the foot of the mountain, sometimes through forests of oak and beech and walnut trees, sometimes between olive orchards and vineyards. Presently it struck across the plain to Foligno,[7] a busy town lying flat in the valley.

In the square of Foligno, Francis had often stood with his father, selling goods at the fairs. Today he held his head high as he rode through the familiar market place.

He thought, "I shall come back a famous soldier, and I will never, never sell things at the fair again."

He blushed with pride when someone in the street pointed him out to a companion, saying, "That young man, who is dressed and mounted like a lord, is the son of Messer Piero Bernardone, the merchant."

At Foligno the company halted to eat and drink and

6. *Spoleto* (spô lā′tô).   7. *Foligno* (fô lēn′yô).

to rest through the hottest hours of the day. When they were in the saddle again and had left the city gates behind them, Francis no longer rode superbly, with his chin in the air. Instead, he went silently, with drooping head, and let his horse lag behind the others along the level stretch of road. He could not himself have told what was the matter. Nothing had happened; the woods were as green and the sunshine as bright as in the morning, but he who had been so proud and gay a few hours earlier felt strangely weary and sick at heart. He lingered to let his horse drink from the clear little river that comes dancing down from the mountain and glitters across the plain, but not even the song of the water made him merry. His comrades noticed his silence, but they were all too deeply interested in their own plans and hopes to think of anything else.

In the late afternoon they entered the glorious oak forest that filled the ravine where Spoleto lies at the end of the Umbrian valley. Beyond, their way would be through a narrow mountain pass where, over and over again, armies had fought fiercely to hold the road to Rome. Deep in the cool woods, the birds were singing and, for the first time in his life, it seemed to Francis that they sang not joyfully, but sadly.

Perhaps he had not grown strong after his long imprisonment, and so could not bear the fatigue of the hard saddle ride. Whatever the reason may have been, it is certain that, when the party reached Spoleto, Francis took to his bed with fever, and that his companions rode on the next day without him.

And Francis had no wish to follow them. There had come upon him a great horror of a soldier's life. As he lay burning with fever and sleepless with pain, all his dreams of glory faded. Instead of knights with shining armor and bright banners, he seemed to see women weeping, little children begging for bread, beautiful cities ruined and desolate.

We do not know how he made his way home. It was a strange and sorry journey, and, at the end of it, he met with ridicule from those who had seen him ride away so bravely to seek his fortune as a soldier. But if his thoughtless friends mocked him, and his father and brother reproached him, his mother was glad to welcome and to care for him. Perhaps she, alone, understood the change in him.

The first days after his return were the most sorrowful that Francis had ever known. Though he was sure that he had decided rightly, it pained him to know that his friends thought him weak, or, perhaps, even cowardly. Besides being hurt, he was puzzled, not knowing what he should do next. A week ago his path had lain clear before him, like the white road in the valley; now it had lost itself in a tangled forest.

We do not know how long his trouble lasted, or what he was doing in these dreary weeks; but we know that, by and by, he began to see plainly again, and all his doubts and puzzles vanished. It was as if he had found his way through the forest and saw the path that he must take, a narrow path and rough, a lonely path, but straight to follow.

He did not know that in a few years hundreds of fellow-travelers were to come and ask that they might walk with him along that narrow way; that instead of being, as he had dreamed he might, Francis Bernardone, the most famous knight in Italy, he should become Brother Francis, the man who loved God, and whom all men loved. All that Francis knew was that, in place of his old love for a soldier's life and his old desire to become a great prince, had come a new love and a new desire—a love for all the ragged and hungry and sick and sorrowful folk in the world, and a desire to feed, and clothe, and heal, and comfort them all.

The Sermon of Saint Francis

HENRY WADSWORTH LONGFELLOW

Around Assisi's convent gate
The birds, God's poor who cannot wait,
From moor and mere[1] and darksome wood
Come flocking for their dole of food.

"O brother birds," Saint Francis said,
"Ye come to me and ask for bread,
But not with bread alone today
Shall ye be fed and sent away.

"Ye shall be fed, ye happy birds,
With manna of celestial words;
Not mine, though mine they seem to be,
Not mine, though they be spoken through me.

"Oh, doubly are ye bound to praise
The great Creator in your lays[2];
He giveth you your plumes of down,
Your crimson hoods, your cloaks of brown.

1. *mere:* a lake or pool.   2. *lays:* songs.

"He giveth you your wings to fly
And breathe a purer air on high,
And careth for you everywhere,
Who for yourselves so little care!"

With flutter of swift wings and songs
Together rose the feathered throngs,
And singing scattered far apart;
Deep peace was in Saint Francis' heart.

He knew not if the brotherhood
His homily[3] had understood;
He only knew that to one ear
The meaning of his words was clear.

3. *homily:* sermon.

The two towers of the Cathedral of the Virgin of the Pillar
rise above the city of Saragossa and above the barren gray hills.
Below it flows the Ebro River which once divided the empire
of Charlemagne the Great from that of the Moorish sultans.
From the first century a chapel to the Virgin has stood here
in this ancient kingdom. For here, say the Spaniards,
Saint James the Apostle, the patron saint of Spain, first preached
the Gospel. Here, too, he beheld a vision of the Virgin.
She stood upon a stone pillar which, in centuries to come,
would be enclosed within this great cathedral.
A constant procession passes through this shrine at Saragossa.
The queens of Spain and the lowliest peasants have bowed
before the Queen of Heaven.
Below the great dark dome the faithful say the

Prayer of the Pilgrims at Saragossa

Virgin most powerful, loving helper of the Christian people, what great thanks we owe thee for the assistance thou didst give our fathers, who, when they were threatened by the infidels, invoked thy help by the devout recitation of the Rosary.

Rise, then, O Mary, hear now the prayers of the whole Christian world, and banish those who, in their insolence, blaspheme Almighty God and would destroy His Church.

Castles in Spain

HENRY WADSWORTH LONGFELLOW

How much of my young heart, O Spain,
Went out to thee in days of yore!
What dreams romantic filled my brain,
And summoned back to life again
The Paladins[1] of Charlemagne,
The Cid Campeador[2]!

White crosses in the mountain pass,
Mules gay with tassels, the loud din
Of muleteers, the tethered ass
That crops the dusty wayside grass,
And cavaliers with spurs of brass
Alighting at the inn;

White hamlets hid in fields of wheat,
White cities slumbering by the sea,
White sunshine flooding square and street,
Dark mountain ranges, at whose feet
The river beds are dry with heat,—
All was a dream to me.

How like a ruin overgrown
With flowers that hide the rents of time,
Stands now the Past that I have known,
Castles in Spain, not built of stone
But of white summer clouds, and blown
Into this little mist of rhyme!

1. *Paladins* (păl'à dĭnz): officers of the palace.   2. *Cid Campeador* (sĭd kăm pā'à thōr): the chief commander; in Spanish literature, the title of a champion of Christianity.

The Little Bells of Sevilla

DORA SIGERSON SHORTER

The ladies of Sevilla go forth to take the air,
They loop their lace mantillas, a red rose in their hair;
Upon the road Delicias their little horses run,
And tinkle, tinkle, tinkle, the bells go every one.

Beside the Guadalquivir, by orange-scented way,
The ladies of Sevilla they come at cool of day;
They wave their fans coquettish, their black eyes gleam
and glow,
And all their little carriage bells a-jingle, jingle go.

There, too, the caballeros drive in the scented breeze,
Upon the road Delicias among the flowering trees;
Beneath their brown sombreros their dark eyes flame and
flash,
And all their little horses' bells right merrily they crash.

Beside the Guadalquivir the hours are very fair,
The nightingale is tuning upon the scented air;
Oh, laughing Andalusia, beloved of the sun,
Your merry, merry little bells, they call me every one.

Home to Avila

KATHERINE RANKIN

All the way eastward through old Spain, past silvery olive trees and wasteland bright with yellow rockflowers, Teresita waited for the moment she would again see the walls and towers of Avila.[1]

Ever since the long sea voyage from Peru ended at the Spanish port of San Lucar, she had watched with eager eyes and racing heart for the castle she called home.

Through the years she had spent in the New World, Teresita had listened to her father's homesick stories of Avila, the birthplace she had been too young to remember. Her brothers could recall every room, every corner, every turret, but Teresita knew only that the palace in Spain had sheltered many generations of her proud people.

Avila! There Spanish gentlemen were the noblest, Lorenzo de Cepeda[2] would tell the child; there Spanish ladies were the loveliest. In the great and terrible solitude of the new land her father spoke of the glories of the most lavish court in Europe. For Teresita he built a background of wealth and gaiety and adventure. It made more lonely the life they lived in the wilderness where parakeets shrieked in damp bogs, where monkeys peered with wild eyes from matted jungles.

"Sometime I shall dance in our castle ballroom to the music of guitars," Teresita sighed, as she and her brothers watched Indians labor with hatchet and sword-knife to make a clearing in the dark forest around them.

1. *Avila* (ä'vê lä): a town in Spain.   2. *de Cepeda* (dē thā pā'dà).

"You shall see a bullfight by moonlight," her brother Lorenzo promised her.

"And ride in a painted coach?" she asked.

"It shall be drawn by milk-white Arabian steeds," said her brother Francesco.

"Shall I wear a jeweled comb?"

"And a lace mantilla, and satin shoes, and a velvet gown," said Lorenzo, "for you are a daughter of Spanish nobles."

"Do you think I shall marry a duke?"

Francesco laughed. "The richest duke in Spain," he said.

"And live at Avila?"

"Happily ever after," said Lorenzo.

Often Teresita's father spoke to her of Spain. With dulled eyes, as a man speaks of something lost, he told his daughter of the ancient town of Avila, where Goths and Romans had fought for possession; where Christians had built battlements to defend themselves against the Moors; where the Cid, that great legendary hero of Spain, had passed in triumph; where de Cepedas had lived in the oldest castle whose thick gray walls rose like a fortress above the city ramparts. "All of the men were brave, and all of the women were beautiful," he boasted, as he told of his three sisters and his eight brothers.

"None more brave than you," Teresita said loyally, for she knew, though it was a time of great deeds, that it had taken courage for her father to bring his wife and young children into exile. For now, more than a hundred years after the discovery of America by Christopher Columbus, the throne of Spain was reaping its reward of vision. Mexico had been conquered. The Philippines had been brought into the Spanish empire. The Indies and all their wealth belonged now to Philip the King. "You would not have come to Peru if the king had not begged you to lead one of his expeditions."

"I am proud to serve my king and country," her father said, "and to spread Christianity to the pagans."

"Pagans!" scoffed her brother Lorenzo. "There is more here in Peru than a heathen people. There is gold! The gold of the Incas!"[3]

Always, since the death of her mother a year ago, there had been this conflict between father and son. Dreading it, yet knowing that nothing she could do would quiet the storm, Teresita listened now. "Say no more!" Lorenzo de Cepeda thundered at his first-born child.

3. *Incas* (ĭng′kàz): Indian tribes living in Peru at the time of the Spanish conquest of that country.

"It is true!" the boy hurled back at him. "The Spanish explorer Pizarro[4] showed us how to handle the barbarian. He killed the Inca leader for a ransom. Pizarro did very well here in Lima. So shall I."

Her father turned wearily away. "There are more things in life than gold," he sighed. "There is the salvation of your soul."

"You talk like my Aunt Teresa," sneered the boy.

"Not another word!" the older man warned his son. "My sister is truly a saint—and this family has need of saints!"

Teresita knew a little about her father's sister, who was his favorite and for whom she had been named. Sometimes, in the dark silences of the hot nights, he told her of the dark-haired señorita who once had sung and laughed and danced through the high rooms of the stone-floored palace. This was the girl who, just seven months before her twenty-first birthday, had entered the Carmelite Convent of the Incarnation at Avila.

"It was All Souls' Day," Teresita's father said. "There had been a masquerade in the castle the night before she went away. She dressed as a gypsy. Then she hung her bright tambourine on the wall of her room, and said good-by."

Beyond that he seldom spoke of Sister Teresa of Jesus. Through years of exile in Peru, Teresita learned much of the other members of her father's family, but it was only through her letters from Spain that Teresita learned to know Sister Teresa of Jesus.

For the child would watch for the coming of the

4. *Pizarro* (pĭ zär'rô): the conqueror of Peru.

Spanish fleet into the harbor of Lima. She would wait, breathless with excitement, for the leather-coated messenger with the mail. She would read and re-read letters from far-off Spanish cousins and friends, letters that told of feasts and festivals, of mighty men and noble ladies. Then, to her father, she would turn for the messages from his sister.

The words were always simple. Even when she wrote of high spiritual purpose, Sister Teresa's thoughts were drawn from homely sources:

"If fish are taken from a river in a net they cannot live, and so it is with souls drawn out of heavenly water," she would write; or

"Those who overload their souls with sorrow are like a child burdened with two bushels of corn, who cannot carry but one, and breaks down under the burden"; and

"The sight of fields, of water and flowers, are a book wherein one reads the goodness and greatness of God."

Sometimes Sister Teresa set down news of the Carmelite convents she was founding, and why she was founding them. She had wept bitterly, she said, over the Lutheran heresies that ravaged Germany and France. She felt that face to face with such disaster she should not allow herself a moment's rest. What, however, could be done? She was a woman, and a life of public preaching was forbidden her. A bold idea had presented itself to her mind. She would seek chosen souls anxious to lead a perfect life of poverty and sacrifice. She would found new convents. There the nuns would follow the primitive rule of Carmel. It was reform, she wrote, but Spain had need of reform.

But, to Teresita, longing for the gleam of Spanish grandeur, her aunt seemed unreal. Once she questioned her brothers. "How could she leave home and enter a convent?" she asked.

"Do not ask me," said Lorenzo.

Francesco was silent for a moment. "Perhaps you will understand," he said, "when you are older—and wiser."

Four years later Teresita came back to Spain. On a day when the seaport of San Lucar blazed with color, she set foot upon her native shore. It was a feast day. Guns roared from a garrison on the hill. A great procession of priests, and acolytes, and societies with bright banners was marching through flag-hung streets. After

them the archbishop, his robes glowing in the sunlight, moved solemnly on his way. Soldiers and tradesmen, princes and peasants, knelt in the streets of the port town.

"Say your prayers," her father whispered to Teresita.

She fingered her rosary but, dazzled by old dreams of Spain she wondered, as she rose to her feet, if she would see a bullfight that night before they started on their way up the mountain roads to Avila.

The night was merry. The next few days were even merrier. At every stop of the galloping stagecoach Lorenzo and his sons and Teresita were welcomed by old friends and many, many relatives. Horsemen, their silver spurs glittering, rode joyously for a time beside the speeding coach. Ladies, flowers in their hair, smiled greetings from rug-draped balconies. There was song and laughter all the way from the sea to Avila. For this return, Teresita told herself, she had been waiting all of her life. This was the Spain of her lonely dreams, this land of creaking draw-bridges, of golden gates, of noble ladies dressed in velvet and brocade with jeweled fans and scented handkerchiefs. This was the land of pomp and of power.

She did not even want to listen to the words of a traveler who sat beside her father in the thundering coach. He was a Carmelite Friar, a young man with a high, broad forehead and great dark eyes. "There is a change in Spain since you went away," he was telling her father. "Men are no longer talking of the empire; they are speaking of the deeds of saintly men."

It was her brother Lorenzo, leering from his corner, who shouted reply. "Who are these saints of whom they speak?"

Against her wishes Teresita listened to the friar's stories of Francis Borgia, the Spanish duke who had become a Jesuit; of the gallant young army captain Ignatius Loyola who had hung up his sword in the shrine of Our Lady of Montserrat; of the brave knight Francis Xavier, who had gone off to the far stretches of Asia to carry the message of Christ; of John of the Cross who was leading Spain, the friar declared, into an era of repentance.

Lorenzo de Cepeda turned toward the friar. "My sister Teresa is a Carmelite, like yourself," he said.

"You are a brother of Sister Teresa of the Discalced Carmelites?" the friar cried in amazement.

Teresita's father looked puzzled. "What do you mean, *discalced?*" he asked. "*Discalced* means shoeless. Surely they wear shoes?"

"Shoeless?" cried young Lorenzo.

"Shoeless?" echoed Teresita.

The friar shrugged his thin shoulders. "They wear *alpargartas,*"[5] he said.

"*Alpargartas!* Those are the sandals of Spanish peasants," gasped young Lorenzo.

The friar's austere face lighted in sudden glow. "And they sleep on straw mattresses, and they live on vegetables from their own garden, or food that is passed through the door of their convent by friends," he said.

"Why?" demanded young Lorenzo.

The friar turned to face him. His eyes were blazing. "Because Spain has forgotten that Jesus was poor," he said, "and it is time we returned to His humility."

5. *alpargartas* (äl pär gä′täs).

"But my aunt Teresa—" Teresita protested, remembering the castle and the tambourine on the wall.

"Your aunt Teresa is the greatest saint in Spain." The friar blessed himself. "God be with her, and with all of us."

Only Teresita's father said courteous farewell to the friar as the stagecoach drew up at the de Cepeda castle gate. Neither she nor Lorenzo looked back after they had stepped down into the darkness. For then she forgot her aunt Teresa in the welcome that awaited them. In the softness of the Spanish night the castle torchbearers stood shoulder to shoulder, a guard of honor. They lined the road from the highway to the wide lighted doorway. Back of them, massed in the shadows from the flaring torchlight, were hundreds of townspeople, shouting, singing, laughing, offering noisy greetings to their rich noble who had returned at last from a far new world. It was time of festival. It was no time to think of a girl who had been foolish enough to renounce such glory.

Once, though, in the castle chapel, as Teresita knelt in prayer of thanksgiving for their safe voyage home to Spain, there came a fleeting thought of a dark-eyed girl who once had knelt at this marble altar rail. Had Sister Teresa of Jesus been as beautiful as people said? Had she wandered over the rocks of Avila to find flowers for the Virgin's altar? Had she, perhaps, even dreamed that one day she would marry a tall and handsome young duke?

Many days later, at her father's stern insistence, Teresita carried a basket of food to the door of the Convent of Saint Joseph. Arms outstretched, Sister Teresa was waiting for the girl she had not seen since her infancy.

She held Teresita at arm's length to study her eyes, her height, her hair.

"You are like my dear sister Juana when she was your age," she said, and added, "she was lovely, too."

Teresita responded, rather unwillingly, to the warmth in the smiling nun's voice. "I saw a portrait of you yesterday in Aunt Juana's palace," she said. "It is the one that Fray Juan painted not long ago."

Sister Teresa nodded. "Did you like it?"

Teresita looked into her aunt's merry eyes. "It does not look like you at all," she said. "You look saintly in it, but not sad."

Sister Teresa's laugh rang out in the little room. "God does not like gloomy saints," she said. She flung her arm across the girl's shoulders and led her into the garden. In spite of herself, Teresita looked around with interest. She heard a Sister singing as she washed a window; she heard happy voices from the vegetable patch where other Sisters were hoeing and planting and raking.

"You are all so cheerful here," she said in astonishment.

The surprise in Teresita's voice amused her aunt. "You cannot be unhappy if you pray for others and forget yourself," she said.

"Do you pray all the time?" Teresita asked her.

Sister Teresa of Jesus laughed aloud. "We wouldn't eat if I did," she said. "Sometimes I am the cook. I work in the kitchen."

"The kitchen?" Teresita was horrified, remembering the remote kitchen in the castle on the hill, where an army of silent servants moved quietly to serve the whims of the de Cepedas.

"Next to the chapel, the kitchen is the nicest room in the convent," said Sister Teresa, "for God walks, too, among the pots and pans."

They were both laughing as the young nuns came in from the garden to greet the niece of their Foundress. As Teresita bowed stiffly to Antonia of the Holy Ghost, to Ursula of the Saints, to Mary of the Cross, and to Mary of Saint Joseph, she noted something other than their rough woven dresses and their veils of coarse white linen. In their faces, brighter than the gold of the Incas, she saw contentment. She wondered about this a little later as she walked slowly up the rocky road toward home. Why was it, she mused, that women who gave up the world should miss it so little?

The world, though, with all its jealousies and bitterness, was pounding on the doors of the castle of Lorenzo de Cepeda. Revelry still went on. Visitors came from Madrid, from Burgos, from Salamanca. Mounted horsemen, their saddles studded with gold, vied with each other in contests on the plain. Under the light of the hundred-branched candelabras, the nobles and their ladies danced at a pace that grew swifter and swifter, to music that throbbed with midnight magic. But, underneath its spell, there was the feeling of storm and strife. Even to Teresita, who did not want to heed the storm signals, the drums of doom were sounding.

Sometimes she would hear her father and his friends talking long into the night. The enemies of mighty Spain were threatening to band against her.

Within the castle there was trouble, too. Teresita's father had purchased more land and now he began to regret it, lamenting that he might have gained quicker returns by easier methods.

"Cultivate that land," Sister Teresa of Jesus wrote to him. "Jacob and Abraham and Saint Joachim guarded their flocks, and they were saints. Too many seek money by investment instead of by hard work."

Lorenzo de Cepeda often sought advice, for Sister Teresa of Jesus concerned herself constantly about her brothers, their children, their marriages, their lawsuits, while all the time she prayed for their souls. "It is all very well for me to detach myself from the world," she once said, "but the world pursues me."

About Francesco there was no concern, for Teresita's brother was soon to marry a beautiful girl of noble family. She would bring to the house of de Cepeda a royal name and a large dowry, as well.

Lorenzo, though, had found wild companions.

"He is too fond of pleasure," Sister Teresa told his father. "I love him, but we will have trouble with him."

So, with a wayward son and lawsuits and the troubled times in Spain, anxiety broke down the spirit and health of Lorenzo de Cepeda. Even more than concern for his own troubled affairs, though, was his alarm about Sister Teresa of Jesus.

A fearful storm had swept over her. Now, in her old age, had come her greatest challenge. Violence and treachery had broken out against her reforms. Foreign groups fought the extreme simplicity of her Carmelite rule of absolute poverty. Though she had established seventeen convents in less than twenty years, though she had undertaken long and trying journeys all over Spain, her friends knew that she was in danger now.

"You may be harmed," they warned, knowing that powerful men thought her methods wrong.

"I am not afraid," Sister Teresa comforted them. "My soul would be in a very bad way if it dreaded the truth." But she appealed to the Pope at Rome, to King Philip of Spain, and she set to work to make sure that her Foundations would survive.

Lorenzo de Cepeda paced the floors of the castle. "Pray for her," he begged his daughter.

The girl knelt in the chapel where once Sister Teresa had prayed. She thought of the trials and afflictions that her aunt was passing through to make secure an Order where women might serve God in simplicity and peace. She thought of the sacrifices Sister Teresa had made, of her warm heart, of her generous concern about her relatives, her friends, and the Sisters. Stirred to tears, Teresita prayed, "God forgive the people who seek to harm her!" knowing at last, as she offered her prayers to

Heaven, that, of all her relatives, Sister Teresa was her most beloved.

Teresita, kneeling there, could not bear to think that those golden wings of faith should be clipped by less spiritual souls. Who else in Spain had so endeared herself to her countrymen? Teresita had seen the crowds, waiting for hours to see Sister Teresa descend from her creaking old cart and give them her blessing. She had seen the poor brightened by care and alms. She had seen the sick healed by the touch of those firm hands. Her enemies could not banish Sister Teresa! They could not sentence her to death!

As she knelt beside the blazing candles Teresita recalled that day in Peru when she had asked, "How could she leave home and enter a convent?" Now she thought again of Francesco's reply, "Perhaps you will understand when you are older—and wiser."

She was older and wiser now. For a long time she bent her head in meditation. In the silence of the little chapel her mind traveled up the long hard road that Sister Teresa must have trod to reach her goal of perfection. She had known, as Teresita learned while she prayed, that the soul is satisfied with nothing less than God.

She arose. Her plan was clear. In her lace mantilla and her velvet gown and her satin slippers she walked slowly down the wide stone halls. She looked up only once at the portraits of Spanish dukes and duchesses of a long line of de Cepedas that loomed above her. Then, through the open oaken door, past the herb gardens and the dark cypress trees and the red Castilian roses she passed down the rocky path that led to the Convent of Saint Joseph.

"I have come to stay," she said, as Sister Teresa met her with questioning eyes. "We Cepedas have always stood together. We stand together now."

Teresita, as the convent door closed behind her, could not foresee that one day King and Pope would rise in defense of Sister Teresa of Jesus. She could not tell so soon that the story of her aunt, and of these Sisters she was about to join, would be written in letters of gold. She could not know then that in centuries to come the world would say, "Behold the Carmelites! They lament for all sinners who do not lament for themselves. They have no longer eyes for the world. Here, among them, faith is consoled. Here is a noble simplicity, a liberal poverty, a cheerful patience."

Teresita only knew as Sister Teresa of Jesus led her toward the chapel of Saint Joseph, that she had come home at last, not to a Spain of royal courts but to a shining land of faith and hope, where she would live happily ever after.

Saint Teresa's Book Mark

Let nothing disturb thee,
Nothing affright thee;
All things are passing,
God never changeth;
Patient endurance
Attaineth to all things:
Whom God possesseth
In nothing is wanting,
Alone God sufficeth.

In the wide, wet delta country of the Rhone River in France
there is a strange little town. It is called "The Shrine of the Three Marys."
It is a pilgrimage town; for here, according to tradition,
Mary Magdalen with two other Marys of the gospels landed from the Holy Land
to bring Christianity to France.
A few centuries ago all of southern France used to journey yearly
to this little village; but time and tides have made access to it difficult.
Though once it was in the path of the Crusaders it is now shut off
by a wall of sandbars.
Yet pilgrims still travel to it. Most of them are gypsies.
They say the servant of the three Marys was a gyspy woman called Sara.
Now the gypsy caravans cross the low-lying marshes to ask help
from the Mother of Mercy. They say the

Prayer of the Pilgrims at Saintes Marie

O Mary, crowned with stars, without thee what life should we have, who are the children of Adam? Each of us has a sorrow that tries him, a grief that oppresses, a wound that rankles.

All men seek thy protection; they come to thy haven of safety and thy fountain of healing. When the waves rise high in the tempest, it is to thee the mariner turns and prays. The orphan flies to thee, for he sees himself as a plant in a thirsty land, defenseless before the winds of life. To thee the poor offer their supplication when they are in want of daily bread. And not even one of us is left without thy help and consolation. Pray for us, Mary, our Mother.

The Bells of Roncevaux[1]

THOMAS WALSH

[Choirs to be arranged in three voices: high, medium, and low.]

Low You can hear them as you go
While the mules creep higher, higher,
Medium Where the torrents overflow
And each summit lifts a spire;
High Through the vales you hear them soaring
In a silvery chant adoring—
Hark, the bells of Roncevaux!

Medium Lone the proud old abbey stands
Dreaming over lost Navarre;
Low Stony lie the folded hands.
High, medium Stony gaze by lamp and star
They who lit the world of story
With the soul's first glint of glory—
All 'Neath the bells of Roncevaux.

Medium Knightly comrades, row on row
In their mountain shrine, forgotten
By their feudal towns below,—
Low There they lie—Fame's first-begotten—
Medium Helms[2] collapsed and hauberks[3] rust—
Medium, high Dust where all the stars are dust—
All Round the bells of Roncevaux.

1. *Roncevaux* (rôns vō′): a hamlet in the Pyrenees Mountains in Spain. 2. *Helms:* helmets. 3. *hauberks* (hô′bûrks): coats of mail.

Charlemagne, emperor of the west and king of France,
crossed the Pyrenees to make war against the Moor.
At one Spanish fortress the traitor Ganelon betrayed the army
as it moved through the valley. There Roland fought,
and Oliver, and the other legendary heroes
of chivalric romance in

The Great Battle of Roncevaux

SIR GEORGE W. COX

In the morning Charlemagne, the king, arose and
gathered to him his host to return to France to keep the
feast of Saint Michael, and to meet Marsilius, a mighty
leader of the Moors. For Marsilius had sent a message
to Charlemagne, promising to follow him to France, and
there to surrender.

And Ogier[1] the Dane he made captain of the vanguard
of his army which should go with him. Then said the
king to Ganelon, "Whom shall I make captain of the
rear guard which I leave behind?"

Ganelon answered, "Roland; for there is none like him
in all the host."

So Charlemagne made Roland captain of the rear
guard. With Roland there remained Oliver, his dear
comrade, and the twelve peers, and Turpin the archbishop, who for love of Roland would fain go with him,
and twenty thousand proven warriors.

Then said the king to his nephew, "Good Roland, behold, the half of my army have I given thee in charge. See
thou keep them safely."

Roland answered, "Fear nothing. I shall render good
account of them."

1. *Ogier* (ō'jẽr): one of the king's officers.

127

So they took leave of each other, and the king and his host marched forward till they reached the borders of Spain. And ever as the king thought upon his nephew whom he left behind, his heart grew heavy with an ill foreboding. So they came into a province of France and saw their own lands again. But Charlemagne would not be comforted, for being come into France he would sit with his face wrapped in his mantle, and he often spake, saying he feared that Ganelon had wrought some treason.

Now Marsilius had sent in haste to all his barons to assemble a mighty army, and in three days he gathered four hundred thousand men to Roncevaux, and there lay in wait for the rear guard of Charlemagne.

Now when the rear guard had toiled up the rocky pass and climbed the mountain ridge, wearied, they looked down on Roncevaux, whither their journey lay. And behold! all the valley bristled with spears, and the valley sides were overspread with them, as multitude blades of grass upon a pasture. The murmur of the pagan host rose to them on the mountain as the murmur of a sea.

Then when they saw that Ganelon had played them false, Oliver spake to Roland, "What shall we now do because of this treason? For this is a greater multitude of pagans than has ever been gathered together in the world before. And they will certainly give us battle."

Roland answered, "God grant it; for sweet it is to do our duty for our king. This will we do; when we have rested we will go forward."

Then said Oliver, "We are but a handful. These are in number as the sands of the sea. Be wise; take now your horn, good comrade, and sound it; peradventure Charlemagne may hear, and come back with his host to help us."

But Roland answered, "The greater the number, the more glory. God forbid I should sound my horn and bring Charlemagne back with his barons, and lose my good name, and bring disgrace upon us all. Fear not the numbers of the host; I promise you they shall repent of coming here; they are as good as dead already in my mind."

Three times Oliver urged him to sound his horn, but Roland would not, for he said, "God and His angels are on our side."

Yet again Oliver pleaded, for he had mounted up into

a pine tree and seen more of the multitude that came against them; far as the eye could see they reached; and he prayed Roland to come and see also. But he would not. "Time enough," he said, "to know their numbers when we come to count the slain. We will make ready for battle."

Then Archbishop Turpin gathered the band of warriors about him, and said, "It is a right good thing to die for king and faith; and verily this day we all shall do it. But have no fear of death. For we shall meet tonight in Paradise and wear the martyr's crown. Kneel now, confess your sins, and pray God's mercy."

Then the Franks[2] knelt on the ground while the archbishop shrived them clean and blessed them in the name of God. And after that he bade them rise, and, for penance, go scourge the pagans.

Roland ranged his trusty warriors and went to and fro among them riding upon his battle steed, by his side his good sword Durandal[3]. Small need had he to urge them; there was not a man but loved him unto death and cheerfully would follow where he led. He looked upon the pagan host, and his countenance became fierce and terrible; he looked upon his band, and his face was mild and gentle.

He said, "Good comrades, lords, and barons, let no man grudge his life today; but only see he sells it dear. A score of pagans is a poor price for one of you. I have promised to render good account of you. I have no fear. The battlefield will tell, if we cannot." Then he gave the word, "Go forward!" and with his golden spurs pricked

2. *Franks:* the followers of Charlemagne. 3. *Durandal* (dū′rĕn däl).

his battle steed. So, foremost, he led the rear guard down the mountainside, down through the pass into the Valley of Death called Roncevaux. Close following came Oliver, Archbishop Turpin, and the valiant Twelve; the guard pressing forward with the shout "*Montjoie!*"[4] and bearing the snow-white banner of their king aloft.

Marvelous and fierce was the battle. That was a good spear Roland bare; for it crashed through fifteen pagan bodies, through brass and hide and bone, before the trusty ash broke in his hand, or ever he was fain to draw Durandal from his sheath. The Twelve did wondrously; nay, every man of the twenty thousand fought with lion-like courage; neither counted any man his life dear to him. Archbishop Turpin, resting for a moment to get fresh breath, cried out, "Thank God to see the rear guard fight today!" then spurred in again among them. Roland saw Oliver still fighting with his spear and said, "Comrade, draw thy sword," but he answered, "Not while a handful of the stump remains. Weapons are precious today."

For hours they fought, and not a Frank gave way. Wherever a man planted his foot, he kept the ground or died. The guard hewed down the pagans by crowds, till the earth was heaped with full two hundred thousand heathen dead. Of those kings which banded together by oath to fight him, Roland gave good account, for he laid them all dead about him in a ring. But many thousands of the Franks were slain, and of the Twelve there now remain but two.

---

4. *Montjoie* (môn zhwä'): the French word for *Hill of Joy*, the battle cry of the Franks.

Marsilius looked upon his shattered host and saw them fall back in panic, for they were dismayed because of the Franks. But Marsilius heard the sound of trumpets from the mountain top and a glad man was he; for twenty strong battalions of Saracens[5] were come to his help, and these poured down the valley side. Seeing this, the rest of the pagans took heart again, and they all massed about the remnant of the guard, and shut them in on every hand.

Nevertheless Roland and his fast-lessening band were not dismayed. So marvelously they fought, so many thousand pagans hurled they down, making grim jests the while as though they played at war for sport, that their enemies were in mortal fear and doubted greatly if they could overwhelm these men. For it looked as if God's angels had come down to the battle. But the brave rear guard dwindled away, and Roland scarce dared turn his eyes to see the handful that remained.

Then Roland spake to Oliver, "Comrade, I will sound my horn, if peradventure Charlemagne may hear and come to us."

But Oliver was angry, and answered, "It is now too late. Hadst thou but heeded me in time, much weeping might have been spared the women of France, Charlemagne should not have lost his guard, nor France her valiant Roland."

"Talk not of what might have been," said Archbishop Turpin, "but blow thy horn. Charlemagne cannot come in time to save our lives, but he will certainly come and avenge them."

5. *Saracens:* Moslems.

Then Roland put the horn to his mouth and blew a great blast. Far up the valley went the sound and smote against the mountain tops; these tossed it on from ridge to ridge for miles.

Charlemagne heard it in his hall, and said, "Listen! what is that? Surely our men do fight today."

But Ganelon answered the king, "What folly is this! It is only the sighing of the wind among the trees."

Weary with battle Roland took the horn again and winded it with all his strength. So long and mighty was the blast, the veins stood out upon his forehead in great cords. He blew on till with the strain his brain almost broke asunder at the temples.

Charlemagne heard it in his palace and cried, "Hark! I hear Roland's horn. He is in battle or he would not sound it."

Ganelon answered, "Too proud is he to sound it in battle. My lord the king groweth old and childish in his

fears. What if it be Roland's horn? He hunteth per-chance in the woods."

In sore pain and heaviness Roland lifted the horn to his mouth and feebly winded it again. Charlemagne heard it in his palace and started from his seat. The salt tears gathered in his eyes and dropped upon his snowy beard; and he said, "O Roland, my brave captain, too long have I delayed! Thou art in evil need. I know it by the wailing of the horn! Quick, now, to arms! Make ready, every man! For straightway we will go and help him." Then he thrust Ganelon away, and said to his servants, "Take this man, and bind him fast with chains; keep him in ward till I return in peace and know if he have wrought us treason." So they bound Ganelon and flung him into a dungeon; and Charlemagne the Great and his host set out with all speed.

Fierce with the cruel throbbing of his brain, and well-nigh blinded, Roland fought on. The little company that was left of the brave rear guard cut down great masses of the pagans, and reaped among them as the reapers reap at harvest time. Yet where each Frank lay, beside him there lay his pile of slain, so any man might see how dear he had sold his life.

The pagan king espied where Oliver was fighting and spurred his horse and rode and smote him through the back a mortal wound.

Nevertheless Roland for all his pain took Oliver tenderly down from his horse and spake with gentleness, saying, "Dear comrade, I fear me thou art in an evil case."

Oliver said, "Thy voice is like the voice of Roland; but I cannot see thee."

Roland answered, "It is I, thy comrade."

Then Oliver said, "It is so dark I cannot see thy face; give me thy hand. God bless thee, Roland! God bless Charlemagne and France!" So saying he fell upon his face and died.

A heavy-hearted man was Roland; little cared he for his life since Oliver, his good comrade, was parted from him. Then he turned and looked for the famous rear guard of King Charlemagne the Great.

Only three men were left.

Turpin the archbishop, a Count Gaulter, and Roland set themselves together to sell their lives as dearly as they might; and when the pagans ran upon them in a multitude with shouts and cries, Roland slew twenty, Count Gaulter six, and Turpin five. Then the pagans drew back and gathered together all the remnant of their army, forty thousand horsemen and a thousand footmen with spears and javelins, and charged upon the three. Count Gaulter fell at the first shock. The archbishop's horse was killed, and he, being brought to earth, lay there a-dying, with four wounds in his forehead, and four in his breast.

Then Roland took the horn and sought to wind it yet again. Very feeble was the sound, yet Charlemagne heard it away beyond the mountains, where he marched fast to help his guard.

And the king said, "Good barons, great is Roland's distress; I know it by the sighing of the horn. Spare neither spur nor steed for Roland's sake." Then he commanded to sound all the trumpets long and loud; and the mountains tossed the sound from peak to peak, so that it was plainly heard down in the valley of Roncevaux.

The pagans heard the trumpets ringing behind the mountains, and they said, "These are the trumpets of Charlemagne the Great. Behold, Charlemagne cometh upon us with his host, and we shall have to fight the battle again if we remain. Let us rise up and depart quickly. There is but one man more to slay."

Then four hundred of the bravest rode at Roland; and he, spurring his weary horse against them, strove still to shout "*Montjoie!*" but could not, for voice failed him. And when he was come within spear-cast, every pagan flung a spear at him, for they feared to go nigh him, and said, "There is none born of woman who can slay this man." Stricken with twenty spears, Roland's faithful steed dropped down dead. Roland fell under him, his armor pierced everywhere with spear points, yet not so much as a scratch upon his body. Stunned with the fall he lay there in a swoon. The pagans came and looked on him and gave him up for dead. Then they left him and made all speed to flee before Charlemagne should come.

Roland lifted his eyes and beheld the pagans filing up the mountain passes; and he was left alone among the dead. In great pain he drew his limbs from underneath his horse and arose, but scarce could stand for the anguish of his brain beating against his temples. He dragged himself about the valley and looked upon his dead friends and comrades, and said, "Charlemagne will see that the rear guard has done its duty."

Then Roland heard a feeble voice, and turned, and was aware of Archbishop Turpin. Upon the ground he lay a-dying, a piteous sight to see. However, he raised his trembling hands and blessed the brave dead about him.

And when Turpin beheld Roland, his eyes were satisfied. He said, "Dear Roland, thank God the field is thine and mine. We have fought a good fight." Then joined he his hands as though he fain would pray, but soon he was at rest. A lonesome man in the Valley of Death, Roland wept for the last of his friends.

And Roland, when he found death coming on him, took his sword Durandal in one hand, and his horn in the other, and crawled away to a green hillock whereupon four marble steps were built beneath the trees.

Then he took Durandal into his hands and prayed that it might not fall into the power of his enemies. He said, "O Durandal, how keen of edge, how bright of blade thou art! God sent thee by His angel to King Charle-

magne, to be his captain's sword. Charlemagne girt thee at my side. How many countries thou hast conquered for him in my hands! O Durandal, though it grieves me sore, I had rather break thee than that pagan hands should wield thee against France."

Then he besought that God would now eke out his strength to break the sword; and, lifting it in his hands, he smote mightily upon the topmost marble step. The gray stone chipped and splintered, but the good blade broke not, neither was its edge turned. He smote the second step; the blade bit it, and leaped back, but blunted not, nor broke. The third step was of hard gray substance; he smote it with all his might; the step powdered where he struck, but the sword broke not, nor lost its edge.

And when he could no more lift the sword, his heart smote him that he had tried to break the holy blade; and he said, "O Durandal, I am to blame; the angels gave thee; they will keep thee safe for Charlemagne and France!"

Then Roland lay down and set his face toward Spain and toward his enemies, that men should plainly see he fell a conqueror. Beneath him he put the sword and horn; then, having made his peace with God, he lay a-thinking. He thought of his master Charlemagne. He thought of France and his home that was so dear. He thought of his dear maid, Hilda, who would weep and cry for him. Then lifted he his weary hands to Heaven and closed his eyes in death.

Gloom fell; the mists went up, and there was only death and silence in the valley. The low red sun was setting in the west.

The Shepherd Boy of Chartres[1]

GRACE T. HALLOCK

Long years ago a boy named Jean lived near the town of Chartres in France. His father kept sheep, and Jean was the shepherd who took care of them.

It was very exciting to live in the neighborhood of Chartres in those days, because the people were building a great church, a cathedral in honor of the Virgin Mary. Famous artists and masons and glassmakers came from Paris and from places much farther away than Paris—though to Jean it seemed scarcely possible that any place could be much farther away than that—to carve the statues and to lay the stones and to color the glass for the windows. But it was the people themselves who brought in the materials of which their cathedral was to be made.

Not only working people, peasants and shopkeepers and laborers, but even proud and powerful princes all harnessed themselves to heavy wagons and drew to the town huge blocks of stone from the quarries five miles away, wood from faraway forests, and wine and grain and oil from the villages round about to feed the workmen. Everybody, everybody but Jean, or so it seemed to him, was helping to build this house for Our Lady.

Jean could not help. He had to look after his father's sheep. His father was poor. He had no pen for his sheep. He had no place to keep them except the common pasture, and no one to take care of them except his eldest son.

To be in the midst of excitement and yet not be a part of it is hard to bear. Besides, Jean from a tiny boy had

1. *Chartres* (shär'tr').

139

been taught to love Our Lady as he loved his mother. To show his love for his mother he could pick bunches of gay-colored flowers from the fields and send them home by his sister Marie when she brought him his supper. But it seemed to Jean that the Virgin Mary was too high and magnificent a lady to be pleased with simple gifts. He would never dare to lay in the hands of the Queen of France a bouquet of poppies and daisies, warm from his own hand, and was not the Virgin a Queen to whom even the Queen of France bowed low?

The common pasture lay along the road, and over that road passed the great wagons pulled by human beings. Sometimes, so heavy were the loads, it took a thousand people to pull a single cart. Yet, save for the creaking of the wheels over the rough road and the beat of footsteps, Jean heard not a sound from the throng. Sometimes there was a halt for rest or for food. Then the only voices heard were the voices of the priests telling the people that they must live in peace and love with their neighbors.

One evening in the late fall, when the full moon was just beginning to light up the wide plain, a stream of wagons and people halted a little distance from where Jean had picked his night's resting place. The leaders had decided not to push on to Chartres that night, but to make camp by the roadside.

Jean longed to go and be a part, even for a little while, of that great company bent on the service of the Queen of Heaven. He looked around at his sheep. They were tired after their long wandering in search of food and lay close together, the lambs beside their mothers, just outside the circle of light from the fire he had kindled.

"The sheep are safe," thought Jean. "They are asleep and will not waken till the dawn. The fire will guard them, and I shall come back soon."

But just as he took the first step toward the edge of the camp, a long-drawn howl sounded clear above the low, beelike hum of the throng. Wolves! They had grown very bold of late years and at the approach of winter sometimes dared come into the very streets of the towns. In Paris, wolf-hunts were common on nights when the moon was full. A pig tied to a post near the edge of the city was the bait, and when the pack came, hunters with long spears chased the wolves through the streets.

Yes, a wolf-hunt was fine sport. Some apprentice lads left their supper pot stewing on the fire in order to give chase as the howling of the wolf pack grew louder. Jean, who watched them pluck burning sticks of wood from the fire and run shouting across the plain, smiled to himself. Wolves meant only a wakeful night to him, for he had learned that they never came close to a brightly burning fire. He looked around at the stack of firewood he had gathered earlier in the day and threw a few sticks on the already leaping fire. Let the lads have their fun, he thought. They could come to no harm, and as for bringing back a wolfskin, there was small chance of that. Indeed, the twinkle of the torches was growing larger again now. The boys were returning, but without the wolf.

Then a curious thing happened. Breaking out from the shadow of some trees ran a lad into the full moonlight, and on his face was a terrified look. He had dropped his torch and was flying over the ground. Behind him ran a silent gray shadow.

When the other lads saw their friend's danger they closed in, waving their blazing sticks and yelling at the top of their lungs, in a brave attempt to turn the pursuing wolf back. By the bright light of the torches Jean saw the wolf's red tongue hanging out of his mouth, and foam on his long jaws. A mad wolf!

Tearing off his long, loose shepherd's coat, Jean dashed forward just as the apprentice lad sank exhausted to the ground. For one second the wolf dropped back and prepared to leap on the fallen boy, but when he sprang, the soft folds of a shepherd's coat fell over his head, and he and Jean tumbled to the ground together. The other lads and men came running to help, but in the twisting jumble it was hard to tell which was wolf and which was boy. At last Jean managed to throw himself over the wolf's head, which was still wrapped in the coat.

"Rope! Bring rope!" he panted.

Now that friend and foe were sorted out, there were a hundred hands eager to tie the mad animal and drag him off to the nearest stream to be drowned.

"The wolfskin shall be thine," promised one of the men.

Jean hung his head. He was standing now by his own fire, quieting the frightened sheep. "If it please you, sir," he said shyly, "will you sell the skin for me and with the money buy something for Our Lady?"

"That I will!" shouted the man over his shoulder, for he was in haste to see the end of the wolf.

A hand touched Jean on the shoulder, and the shepherd turned with the littlest lamb of the flock in his arms to face the lad he had saved.

"Thank you," said the boy simply.

For a long minute he stood there, printing Jean's face on his memory, for this apprentice was an artist even then. Above one of the doorways of the cathedral of Our Lady of Chartres you may see carved in stone the picture he made of shepherds just like Jean being led by an angel to the cradle of the Holy Child. No one today knows his name, for the artists who worked on Chartres cathedral in the twelfth and thirteenth centuries left no records behind them other than their works.

Jean never was to know this. He went to sleep happily, thinking of the bit of glass for a window, or the yard of cloth for a garment, which the price of the wolfskin would buy. He could not know that he had done honor to Our Lady as few had ever done, in saving the life of an apprentice lad at the risk of his own.

French Peasants

MONK GIBBON

These going home at dusk
   Along the lane,
After the day's warm work,
   Do not complain.

Were you to say to them,
   "What does it mean?
What is it all about,
   This troubled dream?"

They would not understand,
   They'd go their way,
Or, if they spoke at all,
   They'd surely say:

"Dawn is the time to rise,
   Days are to earn
Bread and the midday rest,
   Dusk to return;

"To be content, to pray,
   To hear songs sung,
Or to make wayside love,
   If one is young.

"All from the good God comes,
   All then is good;
Sorrow is known to Him,
   And understood."

One who had questioned all,
     And was not wise,
Might be ashamed to meet
     Their quiet eyes.

All is so clear to them,
     All is so plain;
These who go home at dusk,
     Along the lane.

In Brittany

E. V. LUCAS

In Brittany the churches
     All day are open wide,
That anyone who wishes to
     May pray or rest inside.
The priests have rusty cassocks,
     The priests have shaven chins,
And poor old bodies go to them
     With lists of little sins.

In Brittany the churches
     Are cool and white and quaint,
With here and there a crucifix
     And here and there a saint;
And here and there a little shrine,
     With candles short or tall
That Bretons light for love of Him
     The Lord who loveth all.

Saint Genevieve

ROBERT GORDON ANDERSON

Long ago, back in the fifth century, Genevieve was born in the village of Nanterre,[1] about five miles from the city gate of Paris. It was at the time when terrible attacks were being made upon Gaul[2] from the wild nations to the east of Europe. The child's father, a peasant who would have liked to remain at home and till his farm, went off to battle the enemy who coveted the rich lands of Gaul.

In one of these rare years of quiet, just as if she were too tired of all the earlier strife and struggle and sorrow, Genevieve's mother quietly died. Genevieve was only seven. On the morning after her mother was laid to rest beneath the shade of the peaceful plane trees in the churchyard at Nanterre, the child arose at dawn and went out to tend her father's sheep.

"You are too young," her father protested.

"I am strong," said Genevieve. "I shall tend the sheep now and, when I am grown, I shall care for the sick and the wounded and the poor."

One day, as she walked with the sheep in the grasses of the Valerien hill, she saw a coach on the road below her. Closer and closer it came, the horses clop-clop-clopping in the heat of the early spring day on the highway that led toward Brittany and the sea.

"It is the bishop," she cried, as she slid swiftly down the hill and sped toward the village. "It is the good Bishop Germain."

1. Nanterre (nän'tär').   2. *Gaul* (gôl): an ancient country of western Europe. A part of it corresponded roughly to the central part of modern France.

146

Everyone in Nanterre knew of the greatness of Bishop Germain. Born the son of wealthy parents, he had renounced wealth that he might take up the Cross and follow Christ. Some of the villagers had even seen the church of the bishop in Paris, the church on the right bank of the River Seine whose porch ceiling was painted a gleaming heaven blue that was bright with golden stars.

In Nanterre they knew Bishop Germain. They knew that he was great not only in his native land, but that even now he was riding toward the ship that would carry him to Britain. Wasn't there heresy in Britain? Hadn't Pope Celestin at Rome sent the good bishop to combat the false doctrines across the channel?

The bishop had already dismounted at the churchyard when Genevieve reached the foot of the hill. She could only kneel outside the church door, for within the church were friends and relatives and neighbors who crowded its narrow space. She was still kneeling as the bishop, attended by the village priest, came out.

"This is little Genevieve," said the village priest. "She has always been dear to us but now, because of her mother's death, we love her all the more."

The bishop smiled down at her. "For what do you pray?" he asked her.

She looked up at his majestic face and, as though she saw ahead of her that day when she would become the savior of Paris, she softly told him, "I want to do great deeds for the honor and glory of God."

No one knows whether or not the bishop sensed the bright and powerful quality of leadership in the little kneeling girl that day. All that they tell in Nanterre now

is that Bishop Germain leaned down and gave Genevieve
a small copper medal. Upon the medal was engraved a
cross. "Pray and work, and learn all the useful skills,"
he said, "and then, with God's blessing, come to Paris."

Genevieve tended her father's sheep. She carded and
spun the wool. She said her prayers. She took a vow of
virginity. She listened to the news from Britain. There
Bishop Germain was preaching to the faithful not only
in the churches, but at the crossroads and in the fields.
Then, when the forces of the heretics moved down from
the north against him, he and the faithful marched into
battle. As they marched they sang out *Hallelujah! Hallelujah!* until the neighboring mountains flung back the

echo and the superstitious savages fled. Even in far-off Nanterre, Genevieve knew that this day was called the *Victory of the Hallelujah*, and that it had been a victory won without a drop of bloodshed.

Before Bishop Germain returned to France, Genevieve's father was dead. With loneliness in her childish heart, this girl of eight went to the city on the Seine to live with her godmother. Paris! She could not know that she was to become its patron saint, that she would not leave this beloved city for seventy-two years, and that through stormy centuries Paris would never lose memory of her.

When the bishop came back to the Paris church with the blue ceiling, she was waiting for him. From that time their interests never clashed. He was content, even proud, when she became a greater personage and saint than he, for true saints never worry about their own sainthood or the honors they receive.

From her entry into Paris, then, at the age of eight, she spent all the time she could take from her studies and prayers to tend the sick, the crippled, the poor. She was twenty-five when Attila[3] and his Huns came, and already she had built a fine hospital and called it "The Hospital of God." It stood beside the long church of Saint Etienne,[4] and it was a good place for a hospital.

But the Huns were at the gates of Paris! Several hundred thousand barbarians, their short legs swung over small horses, had already reached Châlons.[5] Frightened messengers clattered over the one bridge with their news that the oncoming horsemen would ride, once the'

3. *Attila* (ăt'ĭ là): the leader of the Huns, a fierce tribe of barbarians. 4. *S Etienne* (sǎn tā'tyĕn).   5. *Châlons* (shà'lôn').

passed the bridge gate, past the Forum and right up to the hospital within the shadow of the wall of Saint Etienne.

By this time half the population of Paris was calling for the saintly virgin Genevieve to help them. She came out of the hospital. She led the citizens toward the church and, when the litany of supplication was over, she marched at their head past the palace, past the prison, toward the north bridge. Below her the Parisians massed, some already armed, others in everyday smocks and aprons. She climbed the narrow stone treads and came out on a parapet of the only bridge that led into the city.

She knew that Roman legions were at that moment riding to aid in the defense of Paris. She had heard that Gaul's old enemies, the Visigoths, were rushing up from the south to fight Attila. Another doubtful friend was Merovée the Frank; Merovée and his merry, murderous men who had laid waste the cities of Belgium, but who now might help Paris in her hour of need. Compared to the Huns, even the Romans and the Goths and the Franks seemed like friends.

"We are lost," sobbed the citizens of Paris. "We must seek refuge elsewhere. We can never defeat Attila."

"You are not lost," Genevieve hurled at them, "but you must fight."

"It's easy for you to talk," taunted one citizen in a dirty smock.

Without even one look at the Valerien hill where she had so long ago tended her sheep, Genevieve stepped down from the parapet. "To Châlons!" she cried, and she marched at the head of the Parisians toward the plain.

When her little Paris army came to Châlons, they saw Attila's men spread thickly over the fields to the east as far as the eye could reach. There Attila waited with his army, their swords, spears, and javelins poised and ready for action. At dawn he attacked. All over the plain, far and near, the Huns fell on Visigoths to the south; on Parisians to the center; and on the army of the Franks under Merovée to the north. The little barbarian horsemen charged all over the plain as Attila, the flat-nosed, deep-chested king with the blazing eyes, whirled and pounded with his army.

But, in the evening, this little-legged Hun, scourge, fox and despot, paced in royal anger up and down under the stars by the campfires. He upbraided his officers. He cursed his men. At another dawn they mounted, charged, closed in their ranks, retreated, charged again.

But the countercharges came even faster. Franks, Visigoths, Romans, men from Paris—and, on the sidelines, Saint Genevieve—were allies now. The Huns had come out of Asia, driving ahead of them other barbarian tribes. Now it was their turn to flee. It was a new and bitter experience for Attila. Suddenly, leaving half of his little yellow horsemen behind, and digging his heels into the flanks of his wearied pony, Attila fled.

Soon at home, on the isle of old Saint Etienne, Genevieve and all of Paris with the returning heroes, celebrated with a grand *Te Deum* which rang out in triumph over the Seine.

Peace settled down on Paris for a while. Genevieve kept up her works of mercy on mean, gray, narrow streets. On the sick and poor she continued to wait, and let the kings wait—on her. Merovée, because of the help he had given to her in winning victory over the Huns, now sought entrance to the city of Paris.

Genevieve would not permit the heralds to open the city gates. She stood once more and shouted defiance. For a quarter of a century, even in 476, twenty-five years after the battle of Châlons when Rome fell and Paris lost her protector and needed a new one, Genevieve still kept the kings waiting. Merovée lay in his tomb. His son, Childeric, reigned in his stead, and Genevieve was old and as gray as the somber streets of the left bank of the Seine. Her spirit, though, was forever young. "Childeric cannot enter the gates of Paris until he is baptized," she thundered.

Childeric would not pay the price.

After him came a greater king. This was Clovis.

"Like grandfather, like father, like son," Genevieve told his ambassadors. "Clovis knows the condition I demand. No baptism, no city!"

Clovis threw back his head and laughed.

There came a time, though, when his laugh did r
out. For Genevieve had found an ally. Not amon,
but among women. Queen Clotilde, wife of Clovi
not like his blasphemy, for Queen Clotilde, before her
riage to Clovis, had been converted. And since kings,
all men, will listen to their wives only when thing,
wrong, Clovis decided to try Clotilde's idea. Very gi
ually and slowly he turned toward Christ. He was i
transformed in a day. He was a strange, a bloody sort
Christian, but he did come to believe in Christ and, i
that belief, earned the land that swords could not conquei

Genevieve led him to the golden altar of Saint Etienne
as another *Te Deum* rang out over the city and the river
and across to the hills.

Many a war has come since then to Paris. Many a tide
of battle has swung toward the north bridge since they
carried their shepherdess up the hill to where she was
buried in the Church of the Apostles. But not an hour,
not a minute of any day in the year passes without some
child of Paris, old or young, kneeling at her tomb. And
each year, on the night of the third of January, they take
her out of the chapel to circle aisles and nave on the
shoulders of mechanics and postmen, nobles and university professors, while fine ladies of wealth and poor char-
women chant their humble homage.

So, too, whenever danger comes for France, Genevieve
is taken on the shoulders of some of the sons of Paris, and
again she circles the streets of the city she loved and which
she still seems to guard.

Abridged

Paris in Spring

SARA TEASDALE

The city's all a-shining
    Beneath a fickle sun,
A gay young wind's a-blowing,
    The little shower is done.
But the rain-drops still are clinging
    And falling one by one—
Oh, it's Paris, it's Paris,
    And spring-time has begun.

I know the Bois¹ is twinkling
    In a sort of hazy sheen,
And down the Champs² the gray old arch
    Stands cold and still between.
But the walk is flecked with sunlight
    Where the great acacias lean,
Oh, it's Paris, it's Paris,
    And the leaves are growing green.

The sun's gone in, the sparkle's dead,
    There falls a dash of rain,
But who would care when such an air
    Comes blowing up the Seine?
And still Ninette sits sewing
    Beside her window-pane,
When it's Paris, it's Paris,
    And spring-time's come again.

1. *Bois* (bwà): a large, wooded park in Paris.   2. *Champs:* referring to Champs Elysées (shäN zå lē′zā′): a very famous avenue in Paris.

154

Three hundred years ago Saint Joseph Calasanctius died at Rome.
There, in his lifetime, he had gathered poor boys and girls
from the streets and, for them,
opened the first public free school in Europe.
In Vienna, members of a congregation he founded
have carried on his humane work. In charity and justice
they established trade schools. They built homes for workingmen.
They opened a public library. They compiled a prayer book
for workingmen. They sponsored workers' associations.
They erected a shrine and a church to Mary,
Help of Christians.
There the saint, who was a true friend of the poor, is honored
as men and women who live in the shadows of what
was once the most festive city of Europe say the

Prayer of the Pilgrims at Vienna

Let us offer praise and thanksgiving to the Most
Holy Trinity, who hath shown us the Virgin Mary,
clothed with the sun, the moon beneath her feet, and
on her head a mystic crown of twelve stars.

We, the apprentices and workingmen of Christian
homes, offer this prayer of Saint Joseph Calasanctius,
to implore thy patronage.

How the Great Guest Came

EDWIN MARKHAM

Before the Cathedral in grandeur rose,
At Ingelburg where the Danube goes;
Before its forest of silver spires
Went airily up to the clouds and fires;
Before the oak had ready a beam,
While yet the arch was stone and dream—
There where the altar was later laid,
Conrad the cobbler plied his trade.

Doubled all day on his busy bench,
Hard at his cobbling for master and hench,
He pounded away with a brisk rat-tat,
Shearing and shaping with pull and pat,
Hide well-hammered and pegs sent home,
Till the shoe was fit for the Prince of Rome.
And he sang as the threads went to and fro:
"Whether 'tis hidden or whether it show,
Let the work be sound, for the Lord will know."

Tall was the cobbler, and gray, and thin,
And a full moon shone where the hair had been.
His eyes peered out, intent and afar,
As looking beyond the things that are.
He walked as one who is done with fear,
Knowing at last that God is near.
Only the half of him cobbled the shoes:
The rest was away for the heavenly news.

It happened one day at the year's white end,
Two neighbors called on their old-time friend;
And they found the shop, so meager and mean,
Made gay with a hundred boughs of green.
Conrad was stitching with face ashine,
But suddenly stopped as he twitched a twine:
"Old friends, good news! At dawn today,
As the cocks were scaring the night away,
The Lord appeared in a dream to me,
And said, 'I am coming your Guest to be!'
So I have been busy with feet astir,
Strewing the floor with branches of fir.
The wall is washed and the shelf is shined,
And over the rafter the holly twined.
He comes today, and the table is spread
With milk and honey and wheaten bread."

His friends went home; and his face grew still
As he watched for the shadow across the sill.
He lived all the moments o'er and o'er,
When the Lord should enter the lowly door—
The knock, the call, the latch pulled up,
The lighted face, the offered cup.
He would wash the feet where the spikes had been;
He would kiss the hands where the nails went in;
And then at the last would sit with Him
And break the bread as the day grew dim.

While the cobbler mused, there passed his pane
A traveler drenched by the driving rain.
He called him in from the stony street
And gave him shoes for his bruised feet.

157

The traveler went and there came a crone,
Her face with wrinkles of sorrow sown.
A bundle of fagots bowed her back,
And she was spent with the wrench and rack.
He gave her his loaf and steadied her load
As she took her way on the weary road.
Then to his door came a little child,
Lost and afraid in the world so wild,
In the big, dark world. Catching it up,
He gave it the milk in the waiting cup,
And led it home to its mother's arms,
Out of the reach of the world's alarms.

The day went down in the crimson west
And with it the hope of the blessed Guest,

And Conrad sighed as the world turned gray:
"Why is it, Lord, that your feet delay?
Did You forget that this was the day?"
Then soft in the silence a Voice he heard:
"Lift up your heart, for I kept My word.
Three times I came to your friendly door;
Three times My shadow was on your floor.
I was the traveler with bruised feet;
I was the woman you gave to eat;
I was the child on the homeless street."

Four Things

HENRY VAN DYKE

Four things a man must learn to do
If he would make his record true:
To think without confusion clearly;
To love his fellow-men sincerely;
To act from honest motives purely;
To trust in God and Heaven securely.

Where Love Is, There God Is Also

LEO TOLSTOY

In a little town in Russia there lived a cobbler, Martin by name. He had a tiny room in a basement, the one window of which looked out on the street. Through it one could see only the feet of those who passed by, but Martin recognized the people by their boots. He had lived long in the place and had many acquaintances. There was hardly a pair of boots in the neighborhood that had not been once or twice through his hands, so he often saw his own handiwork through the window. Some he had resoled, some patched, some stitched up, and to some he had even put fresh uppers. He had plenty to do, for he worked well, used good material, did not charge too much, and could be relied on. If he could do a job by the day required, he undertook it; if not, he told the truth and gave no false promises; so he was well known and never short of work.

Martin had always been a good man; but in his old age he began to think more about his soul and to draw nearer to God. From that time Martin's whole life changed. His life became peaceful and joyful. He sat down to his task in the morning, and when he had finished his day's work he took the lamp down from the wall, stood it on the table, fetched his Bible from the shelf, opened it, and sat down to read. The more he read the better he understood, and the clearer and happier he felt in his mind.

One morning he rose before daylight, and after saying his prayers, he lit the fire and prepared his cabbage soup and buckwheat porridge. Then he lit the brass urn, or samovar, put on his apron, and sat down by the window to his work. He looked out into the street more than he worked, and whenever anyone passed in unfamiliar boots he would stoop and look up, so as to see not the feet only but the face of the passer-by as well. A house-porter passed in new felt boots; then a water-carrier. Presently an old man came near the window, spade in hand. Martin knew him by his boots, which were shabby old felt ones. The old man was called Stepánitch. He began to clear away the snow before Martin's window. Martin glanced at him and then went on with his work.

After he had made a dozen stitches he felt drawn to look out of the window again. He saw that Stepánitch had leaned his spade against the wall and was either resting himself or trying to get warm. The man was old and broken down and had evidently not enough strength even to clear away the snow.

"What if I called him in and gave him some tea?" thought Martin. "The samovar is just on the boil."

He stuck his awl in its place, and rose; and putting the samovar on the table, made tea. Then he tapped on the window with his fingers. Stepánitch turned and came to the window. Martin beckoned to him to come in and went himself to open the door.

"Come in," he said, "and warm yourself a bit. I'm sure you must be cold."

"May God bless you!" Stepánitch answered. "My bones do ache, to be sure." He came in, first shaking off the snow, and lest he should leave marks on the floor he began wiping his feet; but as he did so he tottered and nearly fell.

"Don't trouble to wipe your feet," said Martin; "I'll

wipe up the floor—it's all in the day's work. Come, friend, sit down and have some tea." Filling two tumblers, he passed one to his visitor, and pouring his own tea out into the saucer, began to blow on it.

Stepánitch emptied his glass, and, turning it upside down, put the remains of his piece of sugar on the top.

"Thank you, Martin," he said, "you have given me food and comfort both for the soul and body."

"You're very welcome. Come again another time. I am glad to have a guest," said Martin.

Stepánitch went away; and Martin poured out the last of the tea and drank it up. Then he put away the tea things and sat down to his work, stitching the back seam of a boot. And as he stitched he kept looking out of the window and thinking about what he read in the Bible. And his head was full of Bible sayings.

After a while Martin saw an apple-woman stop just. in front of his window. On her back she had a sack full of chips, which she was taking home. No doubt she had gathered them at a place where building was going on.

The sack evidently hurt her, and she wanted to shift it from one shoulder to the other, so she put it down on the footpath and, placing her basket of apples on a post, began to shake down the chips in the sack. While she was doing this a boy in a tattered cap ran up, snatched an apple out of the basket, and tried to slip away; but the old woman noticed it and, turning, caught the boy by his sleeve. He began to struggle, trying to free himself, but the old woman held on with both hands, knocked his cap off his head, and seized hold of his hair. The boy screamed, and the old woman scolded.

Martin dropped his awl and rushed out of the door. Stumbling up the steps and dropping his spectacles in his hurry, he ran out into the street. The old woman was pulling the boy's hair and scolding him and threatening to take him to the police. The lad was struggling and crying, "I did not take it. Why are you beating me? Let me go!"

Martin separated them. He took the boy by the hand and said, "Let him go, Granny. Forgive him, Granny."

"I'll pay him out, so that he won't forget it for a year! I'll take the rascal to the police!"

Martin began entreating the old woman, "Let him go, Granny. He won't do it again."

The old woman let go and the boy wished to run away, but Martin stopped him.

"Ask the Granny's forgiveness!" said he. "And don't do it another time. I saw you take the apple."

The boy began to cry and to beg pardon.

"That's right. And now here's an apple for you," and Martin took an apple from the basket and gave it to the boy, saying, "I will pay you, Granny."

"You will spoil him that way, the young rascal," said the old woman. "He ought to be whipped so that he should remember it for a week."

"Oh, Granny, Granny," said Martin, "that's our way— but it's not God's way. If he should be whipped for stealing an apple, what should be done to us for our sins?"

The old woman was silent.

And Martin told her the parable of the lord who forgave his servant a large debt, and how the servant went out and seized his debtor by the throat. The old woman listened to it all, and the boy, too, stood by and listened.

"God bids us forgive," said Martin, "or else we shall not be forgiven. Forgive everyone, and a thoughtless youngster most of all."

The old woman wagged her head and sighed. "It's true enough," said she, "but they are getting terribly spoilt."

"Then we old ones must show them better ways," Martin replied.

"That's just what I say," said the old woman. "I have had seven of them myself, and only one daughter is left." And the old woman began to tell how many grandchildren she had. "There, now," she said, "I have but little strength left, yet I work hard for the sake of my grandchildren; and nice children they are, too. No one comes out to meet me but the children. Little Annie, now, won't leave me for anyone. It's 'Grandmother, dear grand-

mother, darling grandmother.' " And the old woman softened at the thought. "Of course, it was only his childishness," said she, referring to the boy.

As the old woman was about to hoist her sack on her back, the lad sprang forward to her, saying, "Let me carry it for you, Granny. I'm going that way."

The old woman nodded her head, and put the sack on the boy's back, and they went down the street together, the old woman quite forgetting to ask Martin to pay for the apple. Martin stood and watched them as they went along talking to each other.

When they were out of sight, Martin went back to the house. Having found his spectacles unbroken on the steps, he picked up his awl and sat down again to work. He worked a little, but soon could not see to pass the bristle through the holes in the leather, and presently he noticed the lamp lighter on his way to light the street lamps.

"Seems it's time to light up," thought he. So he filled his lamp, hung it up, and sat down again to work. He finished off one boot, and turning it about, examined it. It was all right. Then he gathered his tools together, swept up the cuttings, put away the bristles and the thread and the awls, and taking down the lamp placed it on the table. Then he took the Bible from the shelf. He meant to open it at the place he had marked, but the book opened to another place.

As Martin opened it, he seemed to hear footsteps as though someone were moving behind him. Martin turned round, and it seemed to him as if people were standing in the dark corner, but he could not make out who they were. And a voice whispered in his ear, "Martin, Martin, don't you know me?"

"Who is it?" muttered Martin.

"It is I," said the voice. And out of the dark corner stepped Stepánitch, who smiled and, vanishing like a cloud, was seen no more.

"It is I," said the voice once more. And the old woman and the boy with the apple stepped out and both smiled, and then they vanished.

And Martin's soul grew glad. He crossed himself, put on his spectacles, and began reading the Book just where it had opened; and at the top of the page he read: "I was hungry, and ye gave me meat: I was thirsty, and ye gave me drink: I was a stranger, and ye took me in."

And at the bottom of the page he read: "Inasmuch as ye did it unto one of these my brethren, even these least, ye did it unto me."

Song of the Shepherd Boy

from *Pilgrim's Progress*

JOHN BUNYAN

He that is down needs fear no fall;
  He that is low, no pride;
He that is humble, ever shall
  Have God to be his guide.
I am content with what I have
  Little be it, or much;
And, Lord, contentment still I crave,
  Because Thou savest such.

The Golden Cup of Kazimir[1]

ERIC P. KELLY

On the balcony of a high tower in the old Polish city of Bendzin there stood, on a bright April afternoon, a boy and a girl. They wore the rich clothes of the nobles of that period.

He was dressed in a buttoned velvet coat splashed with trimmings of real gold, knee breeches of the same material, —dark, and caught at the knee with silver clasps,—silk hose, and soft leather sandals that curved up above the toes. She wore a simple loose-fitting dress of white, held by a golden belt at the waist, and over it an unbuttoned short-coat of blue silk, with sleeves puffed at the wrists. She was bareheaded, her light yellow hair falling about her shoulders. Her sandals were of red leather, embroidered with figures.

The castle rose on this side straight up from the water, and below, several hundred feet at least, the waves of a little lake lapped the moss-covered stones. In the middle of the lake, fishing quietly, as if it were not a tragic time in the history of Poland, was old Stanislaus the fool, a half-witted old fellow who worked about the castle.

It was a time of tragedy and terror. The fierce army of Genghis Khan[2] had come from the great empire in the East and had poured into Europe. Russia lay crushed by the attacks of these hard-fighting Tartars. Eighteen large provinces and their capitals had been laid waste. Poland, too, was in danger.

1. *Kazimir* (kä'zĭ mēr): a famous ruler of Poland.   2. *Genghis Khan* (jĕn'gĭz kän'): a fierce Asiatic war lord.

So many men had been killed that none was left to work in the fields. Thousands upon thousands of the dead laid in roadways, through which, day and night, thundered the chariots drawn by the camels and the horses of the invading enemy.

It was the end of the world, some said. It was the downfall of civilization. Poles had died bravely and now, just two days before, the fathers of Stefan and his cousin Elzbietka[3] had ridden away to defend the nearby city of Czestochowa.[4]

In the castle Stefan and Elzbietka had been together for several weeks, for when the girl's father had joined forces with the duke, Stefan's father, he had left his motherless child in the castle, believing that there she would be safe.

"Are the Tartars near?" asked Elzbietka quietly.

"I do not know," said Stefan, "for we have not much gold. There is little here for them to steal."

"But the Cup of Kazimir," she cried. "Have they never heard of that?"

3. *Elzbietka* (ĕls byĕt′kȧ): the Polish name for Elizabeth. 4. *Czestochowa* (chĕn stô hō′vȧ): a city in Poland.

"Perhaps they never have," he answered. Then, hand in hand, they went to look at that wonderful cup of gold set about with precious stones. A marvelous thing, it was famous throughout Poland. It rested in a little hollow in the chapel wall, a place that might have been made for the statue of a saint. Through the chapel windows of stained glass streamed colored rays lighting the altar, lingering upon the silver eagle above it, and striking directly on this precious, gleaming Cup.

"The inscription is in Latin," whispered Stefan. "It says, 'Blest be the Lips that Drink from Me.' It came as a present from the first Kazimir when the first of my ancestors lived in this castle."

The boy and girl went out into the passage again, their eyes still shining as they thought of the beauty of the Cup.

Throughout the great castle a sense of safety reigned. The Tartars would never come to Bendzin. Down in the kitchen, where fowls roasted on the spits in the charcoal, there was much merrymaking. The master was away! The Tartars were at a safe distance! At that very moment the cook's helpers were throwing soot at one another, plastering the walls, and greeting each soldier of the guard with handfuls of the black stuff as he showed himself at the kitchen door.

"Stay!" shouted Stas, the kitchen master, holding his fat sides and roaring with laughter, for they were careful not to throw any soot at him. "Stop this nonsense and get about the kitchen business." Then, catching the nearest boy, he boxed his ears with a will. "Let that soot-box alone."

The soot-box! That was where the mischief started. It stood by the side of the open ovens, high as a man's waist, and nearly full of the soot which was taken weekly from the chimneys. Then, with good-natured shouts, Stas and the cooks and the kitchen boys began to prepare the evening meal.

It grew dark. Torches were lighted in the narrow corridors; tall candles flamed in the great room. Musicians played their instruments, while the captain of the guard sat and dined with Stefan, Elzbietka, and their attendants.

Suddenly there was a cry from the guards. "Tartars!" Surely that was a death cry, and there was the sound of galloping oncoming horses. "To arms!" rang out the alarm, as guards and watchmen thundered out into the castle yard, seizing their armor and weapons as they ran.

Oh, fatal day that saw the castle at Bendzin, which had never fallen before an enemy, stripped of its bravest men! Fatal day when, trusting to its stout walls and gates, men rode away to fight at another place! They thought that their castle would never be harmed. Had they forgotten that all men knew that in Bendzin was one of the most precious treasures in all Poland, the golden Cup of Kazimir?

To make matters worse, the guards at the gate had made a grave error. Supposing themselves safe, never dreaming of an attack, they had let down the drawbridge, expecting to admit their master and his men. But when the first of that terrible company of Tartars galloped into the light of the gate the guards saw their mistake. Numb with surprise and horror, they vainly tried to raise the drawbridge, but before they could do so the light horses of the East were crossing it. On in they dashed like· a pack of wolves and darted through the undefended gate beyond and into the castle yard, where they battled with a few soldiers who struggled to keep them out of the castle itself.

When the first terrible cry of "Tartars!" came from the outside, the captain of the guard rushed away from the table to join his men.

Stefan sprang to the window on the side of the drawbridge. "It is true," he told Elzbietka, in as calm a tone as he could command, "the Tartars are already in the castle yard and may be here at any moment." His heart was pounding like thunder in his ears. "Elzbietka, you must not stay here any longer."

She looked up at him, proud that she saw in him at that moment of danger the courage that made Poland great. "Stefan, I shall stay with you," she said.

He tried to think—failed—and then remembered. "Elzbietka, we must save the Cup of Kazimir. Run to the chapel and take it from its place; then go and tell Stas to hide you, for the Tartars will want food and so will spare the cooks." He drew her toward the door. "Go—go quickly!" he said.

There was battle raging on the stairs. Slight as the delay was, it allowed Elzbietka time to reach the chapel and hasten to the kitchen.

Five minutes later the curtains to the great upper room were pushed aside. A man stood in the doorway. Stefan, turning toward him, sword in hand, gazed in horror, for the man was a Tartar, tall, muscular, dressed in finely finished animal skins and decorated from head to foot with gold,—earrings, neckchains, bracelets, belt,—all taken from the cities he had robbed. Stefan went cold with fear when he saw the man's small dark eyes, his coarse black beard twisted into perhaps a dozen small braids.

"Boy," spoke the Tartar, "tell us where in this castle may be found the Cup of Kazimir, for we are in haste and would soon depart."

Stefan continued to gaze, but did not reply.

"Answer at once," the Tartar snarled at him.

Stefan drew himself up proudly. "I am a Pole," he said, "son of the Duke of Bendzin. Why should I answer?"

"My name," thundered the Tartar, "is Batu, prince of the forces of the Emperor, who is son of the great Genghis Khan. As there is but one sun in the heavens, so shall there be but one ruler on earth, and Batu must be obeyed."

Batu! A name that was dreaded in every kingdom in Europe—a robber second only to Genghis Khan himself in the doing of things cruel and horrible.

Stefan flung back his head. "It is for this moment that I have lived, boy that I am. I, a Pole, refuse to obey your command. You shall not have the Cup of Kazimir while I live."

Suddenly, with an unpleasant smile upon his lips, the smile of one who crowds upon someone weaker than himself, the Tartar advanced upon the boy with his curved scimitar.[5] But he had not counted upon the pride that stiffened Stefan's right hand. One blow Batu struck, not upon the lad, but upon Stefan's beloved sword.

The blade snapped like a reed under the blow, and there remained in Stefan's hand only the jeweled handle and a short piece of broken steel. Then, in a flash, another plan

5. *scimitar* (sĭm'ĭ tẽr): a saber or short sword with a curved blade.

172

occurred to the boy. With all his force he hurled the useless weapon directly into the Tartar's face. It struck the savage upon his dark cheek and Batu staggered under the blow. But only for a moment; then, with the rage of a wild beast, he sprang at the boy. Stefan leaped back. In an instant he was upon the little balcony above the lake, one foot upon the stone railing, and just as the Tartar reached forward to grasp him, the boy flung himself into space.

Old stupid Stanislaus, drifting idly in his boat, saw the brave leap. After he had rescued him and warmed him and wrapped him in his own cloak, the boy cried, as his teeth chattered, "To Czestochowa! Fetch us a cart and horse, Stanislaus, for we must go and find the army."

Then, as they rode, they saw a company of Polish horsemen coming toward them. "See, Stanislaus, see! The White Eagle! They are Poles. They have come in time."

They came nearer. The boy leaped from the cart. A tall rider in full armor, wearing a helmet with a red plume, leaned down from his horse, wondering what peasant boy might be rushing toward him shouting and waving his hands so wildly.

"Father! Father! the Tartars are at Bendzin!" In a moment Stefan was raised to his father's saddle.

Then there went up a great cry through all that throng, "Tartars! The Tartars are at Bendzin! Forward for Poland!" And the dust rose high on the road.

The Poles rode through the still-open drawbridge. They rode toward the silent castle. There was no smoke from the chimneys. There was the silence of death. The Tartars were gone! They had had barely time to seize what gold and jewels they could find and to kill the people of the castle before they dashed on their way.

Stefan, his father, and Elzbietka's father hurried into the kitchen. It was in darkness, and someone came with a torch. What a sight! In the kitchen, heaped with Tartar bodies, lay Stas, the brave cook, his great kitchen knife clasped in his right hand. Everything had been overturned. The Tartars had been hunting wildly for something. And that something Stefan knew to be the Cup of Kazimir. They had not found it in the chapel, then.

More soldiers crowded in as Stefan's father fell upon his knees beside the faithful Stas. Suddenly one of them made a strange sound which caused all to lay hands upon their swords as they looked in the direction in which he was pointing. The hair rose upon their heads at what they saw.

For out of a huge box by the side of the ovens came a figure, small, and hideously black in the torchlight. It was alive, struggling, gasping, trying to speak. For a moment it trembled on the box edge, and then pitched forward on the floor. But when it fell a black mass dropped from its hands and made a clang like metal as it fell. In an instant the nearest soldier had caught up the object, and as he brushed the black away the light fell upon it and made it shine.

"A miracle!" shouted the soldier, "a miracle!"

"The Cup of Kazimir!" cried Stefan, plunging forward and catching it. He did not hold it for an instant. He was down upon the floor brushing the soot from the face of the little black figure. It spoke, *she* spoke; for it was Elzbietka, who had hidden from the Tartars in the kitchen soot-box, the one place they did not think it worth their while to search.

She was covered with soot, half choked, not harmed, though greatly frightened. The night before she had taken the Cup from its place in the chapel and had hurried to the kitchen, where Stas, after hiding her, had lost his life defending her and the precious Cup. For nearly twenty hours she had stayed in the cramped stuffy space, raising her head now and again from the box to breathe more easily.

Her father lifted her in his arms. Still covered with the soot, she was carried upstairs in the midst of the wildest shouting that ever rang through the castle of Bendzin, a shouting that made the roof echo even as does the sky when the thunder peals.

The Polish Pilgrim

KATHERINE RANKIN

I am a pilgrim.
For five days and five nights
I have traveled from my home in the blue mountains
To reach the shrine at Czestochowa,
To pray there to the Black Madonna,
To ask for mercy.
I have come through deep marshes
Where quail and falcon and grouse
Rise in flight at the sound of my wagon wheels;
Above me, because it is May, the larks are singing;
Below me, in the warmth of spring, buttercups are in
    blossom;
For larks sing though cities lie in ruin,
Though towers are crumbled, though homes are in ashes
And buttercups bloom, though men are shot and hanged.
Holy Mary, Mother of God, pray for us!

At dawn I come to the city of the shrine,
The city that has known so many wars;
Hordes of barbarians have fought in this market place;
Charles Augustus, King of Sweden, made these roads a
    battleground;
Napoleon, Emperor of the French, passed here with his
    armies;
Germany has ravaged this land;
Russian regiments, through the years, through the cen-
    turies,
Have stormed this fortress.
Oh, Blessed Lady of Czestochowa,
High above your quiet altar,
The sorrow your pitying eyes have seen,
Your eyes that are as old as time, as old as grief, as old as
    tears!
They call you the Black Madonna
Because Saint Luke the Evangelist

Painted this picture of you upon the dark cedarwood of
   Lebanon,
But you are darkened, too, by the smoke of old battles,
By the scorching flames of the invaders.
Holy Mary, Mother of God, pray for us!

Even ahead of me, in the dawn,
The procession of your Feast has begun;
Thousands of pilgrims are here,
Hundreds of thousands of pilgrims;
They are here from the salt mines, from the oil wells,
They are here from the cherry orchards and the cities;
Bee-farmers, clerks, teachers, fishermen,
Old women, old soldiers, cripples, blind men,
Young boys, girls in their First Communion dresses,
Drummers beating their drums triumphantly,
Trumpeters, with silver voices, calling to you.
Up from the Street of Silence we march,
One group pushing on against the other,
To where the tall wax candles burn
In the soft light, above the roses.
Holy Mary, Mother of God, pray for us!

First pass the children, their voices soft in prayer,
They are young, but no younger than the Eaglets of
   Warsaw,
Who died in the defense of their city.
Then come the wounded soldiers, armless men, and lame,
With the look of battle still deep in ashen faces.
Mother of God, have pity on them!
Behind them are the young girls,
Bright-haired, proud young girls,

As fair and as beloved as the good Queen Jadwiga[1]
Who once prayed that her people might live in peace,
As in the Kingdom of God.
Oh, Blessed Lady, bless them, keep them fair!
Bless the women of Poland!
Bless the men of Poland!
See us now, our rosaries lifted in supplication to you!
Help us, for thou and thy Divine Son alone can help us!
Holy Mary, Mother of God, pray for us!

This is the land of crumbled towers, of broken spires,
This is the land of leveled cities, of violated altars,
This is the land of desolation.
But, oh, Our Lady of Czestochowa, though our land is
    bloodstained,
Though we know hunger and thirst and the fearful after-
    math of war,
We still are proud, proud as the Polish eagle on its field of
    red!
But keep us strong! Fortify us against the evil
That, more terrible than guns and bombs and flames,
Threatens us, derides us, jeers us with its godlessness.
Oh, Blessed Mother, who has looked down through the
    sorrow of your days
Upon the passing ages of this weary world of men,
Fortify us now against the creed of the infidel!
Oh, Black Madonna of Czestochowa, Mother Queen of
    Poland,
Heed us now as you have always heeded us;
Now, in this hour of terror,
Keep for us our freedom! Keep for us our Faith!

1. *Jadwiga* (yäd vē′gà).

Under Northern Skies

The Norse story of creation is the beginning of all Norse legend:

Long ago there was nothing but a gulf of mist. In this mist there was a fountain. Out of the fountain flowed twelve rivers. When the waters of the rivers froze, there was nothing but a field of ice. From a sunnier land to the south a warm wind blew upon the ice and melted it. Clouds were formed and from them came the father of Odin. Odin was king of the Norse gods.

Odin lived at Asgard, the home of the gods. He had a son Thor, who was sometimes called the thunder-god. Odin's wife, Frigg, ruled the sunshine and the rain and the flowers. Then there was Frigg's son, Balder, whom everyone loved, and there was Loki, the god of discord and mischief, whom everyone feared and hated.

The wealth of stories about these gods is to northern countries what the stories of the Greek gods is to the East. It is their racial heritage of literature, of which they are proud.

The gods and heroes of Asgard were in time abandoned for Christianity. It was the great Boniface, years later, who chopped down the Tree of Thor that was still held in reverence by northern pagans. It was Columbanus who went into the pagan lands and brought many pagans into his monastery. It was the Holy See at Rome that converted pagan kings.

Their stories are the literature of northern Europe. For centuries men told these stories. Then the Catholic John Gutenberg devised the art of printing and the stories of the north became the property of the whole reading world.

High above the Gothic door to the old cathedral at Freiburg in Germany
stands a great column that bears aloft a blue-clad figure
of the Blessed Virgin.
Time was on a May Day feast of Our Lady when the great square
in front of the cathedral would be gay with color. Then from the magic depths
of the Black Forest would come peasant women carrying garlands
of field flowers to place at Our Lady's shrine.
Past these banks of primroses and daffodils, marguerites
and lilies of the valley, the white-veiled little girls from the parishes,
the bright-sashed students and seminarians in their dark cassocks
from the universities, the red-robed acolytes, and priests and deacons
and the Archbishop of Freiburg would pass in solemn procession to pay homage
to the Mother of God.
Wars have come and gone in Freiburg; but, through the prayers of her people,
May Day will always remain dedicated to the Blessed Virgin. To her,
they will always say the

Prayer of the Pilgrims at Freiburg

O Lady of the Lilies, help of those who have lost their way, thou hast been proclaimed by holy Church the Comforter of the afflicted. To thee turn the sorrowful in their afflictions, the sick in their maladies, the dying in their agony, the poor in their distress, and those who stand in all manner of need in both public and private calamities. From thee they receive consolation and strength.

Our dearest Mother, turn thy merciful eyes upon us, accept our prayers, and aid us in our spiritual and temporal necessities.

A Legend of the Northland

PHOEBE CARY

Away, away in the Northland,
    Where the hours of the day are few,
And the nights are so long in winter
    That they cannot sleep them through;

Where they harness the swift reindeer
    To the sledges, when it snows;
And the children look like bears' cubs
    In their funny, furry clothes:

They tell them a curious story—
    I don't believe 'tis true;
And yet you may learn a lesson
    If I tell the tale to you.

Once, when the good Saint Peter
    Lived in the world below,
And walked about it, preaching,
    Just as he did, you know,

He came to the door of a cottage,
    In traveling round the earth,
Where a little woman was making cakes,
    And baking them on the hearth;

And being faint with fasting,
    For the day was almost done,
He asked her, from her store of cakes,
    To give him a single one.

So she made a very little cake,
But as it baking lay,
She looked at it, and thought it seemed
Too large to give away.

Therefore she kneaded another,
And still a smaller one;
But it looked, when she turned it over,
As large as the first had done.

Then she took a tiny scrap of dough,
And rolled and rolled it flat;
And baked it thin as a wafer—
But she couldn't part with that.

For she said, "My cakes that seem too small
When I eat of them myself,
Are yet too large to give away."
So she put them on the shelf.

Then good Saint Peter grew angry,
For he was hungry and faint;
And surely such a woman
Was enough to provoke a saint.

And he said, "You are far too selfish
To dwell in a human form,
To have both food and shelter,
And fire to keep you warm.

"Now, you shall build as the birds do,
And shall get your scanty food
By boring, and boring, and boring,
All day in the hard, dry wood."

Then up she went through the chimney,
  Never speaking a word,
And out of the top flew a woodpecker,
  For she was changed to a bird.

She had a scarlet cap on her head,
  And that was left the same,
But all the rest of her clothes were burned
  Black as a coal in the flame.

And every country school-boy
  Has seen her in the wood,
Where she lives in the trees till this very day,
  Boring and boring for food.

And this is the lesson she teaches:
  Live not for yourself alone,
Lest the needs you will not pity
  Shall one day be your own.

Give plenty of what is given to you,
  Listen to pity's call;
Don't think the little you give is great,
  And the much you get is small.

Now, my little boy, remember that,
  And try to be kind and good,
When you see the woodpecker's sooty dress,
  And see her scarlet hood.

You mayn't be changed to a bird though you live
  As selfishly as you can;
But you will be changed to a smaller thing—
  A mean and selfish man.

Prayer of a Child

CHRISTINA ROSSETTI

The Shepherds had an Angel,
The Wise Men had a star,
But what have I, a little child,
To guide me home from far,
Where glad stars sing together
And singing angels are?—

The Wise Men left their country
To journey morn by morn,
With gold and frankincense and myrrh,
Because the Lord was born:
God sent a star to guide them
And sent a dream to warn.

My life is like their journey,
Their star is like God's book;
I must be like those good Wise Men
With heavenward heart and look:
But shall I give no gifts to God?—
What precious gifts they took!

Lord, I will give my love to Thee,
Than gold much costlier,
Sweeter to Thee than frankincense,
More prized than choicest myrrh:
Lord, make me dearer day by day,
Day by day holier.

Epilogue

Out of the cathedrals and cloisters of Europe has come the great literature of the world.

Christian scholars, in thick-walled libraries, preserved the best writings of the ancient Greeks and Romans.

Out of Persia and Mesopotamia, out of Egypt and the lands of the barbarians these learned men of the Church of Christ gathered the great stories. Out of the Old Testament they garnered the sacred traditions of the Jews.

They spread the drama of Paul. They preached the philosophy of Thomas Aquinas. They set in words the ardor of Ignatius, the zeal of Justin. The song chants of Gregory were saved by another Gregory, that Bishop of Milan who gave his wealth to the poor. Augustine, in mighty measures, wrote of the greatness of God. The first standard Bible was translated by the scholar Jerome.

Augustinians, Benedictines, Franciscans, Dominicans created this old-world culture. So did hooded Capuchins. So did black-robed Jesuits. So did the white Carmelites and the Carthusians. So did all the other holy men and women of Europe.

They treasured the beauty of art. They sponsored skill not only in monasteries but among the lay men and women of their time.

They saw the everlasting truth by which man strives to lift himself closer to God.

They lived and they died in beauty, but their work and their tradition remain.

It is our Christian heritage.

Because of it, men still lift their eyes and their hopes toward the divine hills of light.

The Golden City of Saint Mary

JOHN MASEFIELD

Out beyond the sunset, could I but find the way,
Is a sleepy blue laguna which widens to a bay,
And there's the Blessed City—so the sailors say—
    The Golden City of Saint Mary.

It's built of fair marble—white—without a stain,
And in the cool twilight when the sea-winds wane
The bells chime faintly, like a soft, warm rain,
    In the Golden City of Saint Mary.

Among the green palm-trees where the fire-flies shine,
Are the white tavern tables where the gallants dine
Singing slow Spanish songs like old mulled wine,
    In the Golden City of Saint Mary.

Oh, I'll be shipping sunset-wards and westward-ho
Through the green toppling combers a-shattering into
    snow,
Till I come to quiet moorings and a watch below,
    In the Golden City of Saint Mary.

The City of God

SAMUEL JOHNSON

City of God, how broad and far
  Outspread thy walls sublime!
The true thy charted freemen are,
  Of every age and clime.

One holy Church, one army strong,
  One steadfast high intent,
One working ban, one harvest-song,
  One King Omnipotent.

How purely hath thy speech come down
  From man's primeval youth;
How grandly hath thine empire grown
  Of Freedom, Love, and Truth!

How gleam thy watchfires through the night,
  With never fainting ray;
How rise thy towers, serene and bright,
  To meet the dawning day!

In vain the surge's angry shock,
  In vain the drifting sands;
Unharmed, upon the Eternal Rock,
  The Eternal City stands.